FASTING AND PRAYER

A LIFESTYLE OF CONSECRATION

BY

DR. THOMAS L. DRIVER, PH.D., DMIN

© 2026 Dr. Thomas L. Driver, Ph.D., DMIN. All Rights Reserved.
Published by TLDM Evangelistic Media Network

Published by:
TLDM Evangelistic Media Network
https://tldmevangelisticmedianetwork.com/

Cover Design: TLDM Evangelistic Media Network

© 2026 Dr. Thomas L. Driver, Ph.D., DMIN. All rights reserved.

No portion of this publication may be reproduced, stored within a retrieval system, or distributed by any means– electronically, mechanically, through photocopying, recording, or other methods—without obtaining prior written authorization from the copyright owner. The sole exception to this restriction applies to brief quotations used in reviews, articles, or educational works.

Scripture quotations are taken from the **New King James Version® (NKJV)**. Copyright © 1982 by Thomas Nelson. Used by permission. All rights reserved.

Printed in the United States of America.

First Edition.

© 2026 Dr. Thomas L. Driver, Ph.D., DMIN. All Rights Reserved.
Published by TLDM Evangelistic Media Network

Copyright © 2026 Dr. Thomas L. Driver, Ph.D., DMIN
All rights reserved.
Published by TLDM Evangelistic Media Network
Paperback, ISBN: 979-8-9934304-3-0

Dedication

I dedicate this book to the Lord Jesus Christ—my Savior, my Redeemer, my Deliverer, and the One who has sustained me through every season of life.

To the Holy Spirit, my Teacher, Counselor in the wilderness, and my strength through every fast, prayer, and surrender.

To every believer seeking to grow in faith, draw nearer to God, and live with complete surrender—may this book inspire you to experience the remarkable power, clarity, discipline, and closeness that only fasting and prayer can offer.

To everyone who has supported me through challenges, changes, and growth—thank you for your love, patience, and prayers. Your support has uplifted my journey more than words can express.

May this work bring glory to God and inspire future generations to seek Him wholeheartedly.

© 2026 Dr. Thomas L. Driver, Ph.D., DMIN. All Rights Reserved.
Published by TLDM Evangelistic Media Network

Preface

Fasting and prayer have deeply impacted my life in ways words can't fully describe. They have been my anchor through storms, my guide in moments of confusion, and my strength when human effort falls short.

Over the many years of my military service, ministry work, academic studies, business hurdles, and personal wilderness times, I've found that fasting and prayer have played a special role in shaping my character, renewing my vision, and helping me stay aligned with His will.

This book is based on personal experience—not merely theory or research, but on the real journey of walking with God during times that demand spiritual discipline, focus, and unwavering faith.

Fasting became a refuge for me, while prayer offered strength and clarity. Through these practices, I found guidance and healing, and I resisted temptation more effectively, deepening my commitment to Christ.

Over the years, I found that fasting is not just about food; it's about focus. It's an invitation from God to step away from life's noise and return to the simplicity of His presence.

Practices like intermittent fasting, longer fasts, the Daniel fast, and other variations have helped me experience greater spiritual growth, healing, and renewal.

© 2026 Dr. Thomas L. Driver, Ph.D., DMIN. All Rights Reserved.
Published by TLDM Evangelistic Media Network

Every fast brings fresh understanding and highlights how letting go is essential for real change. I hunger for the growth of God, and only a lifestyle of dedication, fasting, and prayer has allowed that for me.

Breaking fasts with Communion was the most meaningful part of my experience. It taught me that fasting is about aligning with Christ, not just self-improvement, and reminded me that my strength comes from my covenant with Him.

This book is written for believers who want more of God. It is for those who hunger for deeper intimacy, clearer direction, stronger discipline, and greater spiritual authority.

Whether you are new to fasting or seeking to deepen your practice, this book will guide you through biblical foundations, practical methods, personal testimonies, and spiritual principles that will transform your life from the inside out.

My prayer is that as you read, the Holy Spirit will stir something within you—a hunger for righteousness, a longing for holiness, and a renewed passion to walk closely with Jesus Christ. May these pages inspire you, strengthen you, and prepare you for the assignments God has placed in your hands.

© 2026 Dr. Thomas L. Driver, Ph.D., DMIN. All Rights Reserved.
Published by TLDM Evangelistic Media Network

Fasting and prayer have changed my life.

I believe they will change yours, too.

—Dr. Thomas L. Driver, Ph.D., DMIN
TLDM Evangelistic Media Network

To God be the glory.

© 2026 Dr. Thomas L. Driver, Ph.D., DMIN. All Rights Reserved.
Published by TLDM Evangelistic Media Network

Contents

Dedication iv
Preface v
Chapter 1: Understanding Fasting: Returning to God with Your Whole Heart 1
    Fasting is Not About Food— It is About Focus 2
    Call to Return to God 4
    My Journey into a Lifestyle of Fasting 5
    Fasting and Prayer: Two Sides of the Same Sword 7
    Fasting is for Every Believer 8
    Guarding the Heart: Fasting is not Performance 10
    Fasting as a Way of Life 11
    Conclusion: Fasting Leads Us Back to God 12
Chapter 2: The Heart Behind Fasting: Place Where Transformation Begins 14
    True Fasting Begins with the Heart, Not the Stomach 15
    Reward of Sincere Fasting 16
    Dependence on God, Not Self-Sufficiency 17
    My Personal Journey: Discovering the Heart of Fasting 18
    Military Heart Transformed by the Spirit 22
    Scholar and Pastor Shaped by Consecration 22
    Fasting Reveals What Needs Transformation 23
    Fasting as Worship: A Living Sacrifice 24

© 2026 Dr. Thomas L. Driver, Ph.D., DMIN. All Rights Reserved.
Published by TLDM Evangelistic Media Network

Expectation: Atmosphere of Breakthrough 25
Conclusion: The Heart Determines the Harvest 26
Chapter 3: Fasting in the Old Testament:
Divine Pattern for Today 28
    Moses: Fasting for Revelation 29
    What Moses Teaches Us 30
    My Reflection 30
    Elijah: Fasting for Renewal 31
    What Elijah Teaches Us 32
    My Reflection 32
    Esther: Fasting for Deliverance 33
    What Esther Teaches Us 33
    My Reflection 34
    David: Fasting for Humility 34
    What David Teaches Us 35
    My Reflection 35
    Daniel: Fasting for Wisdom and Revelation 36
    What Daniel Teaches Us 37
    My Reflection 37
    Isaiah: Fasting for Transformation 38
    What Isaiah Teaches Us 39
    My Reflection 39
    Conclusion: Blueprint for Today's Believer 40

Chapter 4: Fasting in the New Testament: Lifestyle Modeled by Christ and the Early Church 43

   Jesus: Fasting Before Ministry 44

   What Jesus Teaches Us 46

   My Reflection 47

   Jesus' Teaching on Fasting: "When You Fast…"........48

   The Disciples: A Life Shaped by Fasting....................49

   The Early Church: Fasting for Direction and Assignment 49

   What the Early Church Teaches Us 53

   My Reflection 54

   Paul: Fasting as a Lifestyle of Consecration 54

   What Paul Teaches Us...54

   The New Testament Pattern: Fasting + Prayer + Holy Spirit 55

   My Reflection 59

   Why New Testament Fasting Matters Today 60

   Conclusion: Fasting is the New Testament Lifestyle ..61

Chapter 5: Types of Biblical and Practical Fasts: Understanding the Paths God Uses to Transform Us 65

   1. Complete Fast (Water-Only)...................................66

   2. Absolute Fast (No Food or Water) 68

   3. Partial Fast (Restricted Diet) Including the Daniel Fast...72

   4. The One-Meal or Half-Day Fast............................74

5. The 24-Hour Fast or Sabbath Fast 75
6. Intermittent Fasting (or Similar Patterns) 76
Understanding 18:6 and 16:8 Intermittent Fasting 76
7. Specialized Fasts (Bread-Only, Egg-Only, Vegetable-Only, etc.) 80
8. Corporate Fasts (Church, Family, Community) 82
9. Purpose-Driven Fasts (Specific Topics) 83
Conclusion: Your Fast is Your Offering 85

Chapter 6: Preparing for a Fast: Setting Your Spirit, Mind, and Body in Alignment with God 87
1. Preparing Your Heart: The Spiritual Foundation 88
2. Preparing Your Mind: Renewing Your Thoughts 91
3. Preparing Your Body: The Physical Component 93
4. Preparing Your Schedule: Planning for Success 96
5. Preparing Your Spirit Through Scripture 98
6. Preparing with Purpose: Identify What You are Fasting For 98
7. My Personal Approach: Lifestyle of Preparation 99
Conclusion: Preparation Positions You for Victory ... 100

Chapter 7: The Spiritual Power of Fasting: Understanding What Happens in the Unseen Realm 102
1. Fasting Weakens the Flesh and Strengthens the Spirit 103
2. Fasting Increases Sensitivity to the Holy Spirit 104

- 3. Fasting Produces Breakthrough in Spiritual Warfare 106
- 4. Fasting Turns Prayer into Power 108
- 5. Fasting Breaks Chains and Releases Deliverance .109
- 6. Fasting Produces Revelation and Divine Insight ..111
- 7. Fasting Strengthens Spiritual Authority 112
- 8. Fasting Repositions the Believer in God's Perfect Will 113
- 9. Fasting Builds Discipline and Strengthens Character 114
- Conclusion: Unseen Realm Responds When You Fast 115

Chapter 8: Fasting and Prayer: Divine Partnership that Unlocks Breakthrough 117
- 1. Why Fasting Must Always Be Paired with Prayer 118
- 2. Fasting Intensifies Prayer 120
- 3. Fasting Makes Space for God to Speak 122
- 4. Fasting Strengthens Intercession 122
- 5. Fasting Positions You for Breakthrough 123
- 6. Fasting Deepens Worship 125
- 7. Praying the Word During a Fast 127
- 8. Listening Prayer: Most Overlooked Part of Fasting 128
- 9. Journaling Prayer: Capturing What God Reveals .131

© 2026 Dr. Thomas L. Driver, Ph.D., DMIN. All Rights Reserved.
Published by TLDM Evangelistic Media Network

    10. Synergy of Fasting and Prayer 133

Chapter 9: What Happens to Your Body When You Fast: Physical, Mental, and Emotional Benefits of Consecration 138

    1. Fasting Recalibrates the Body 139

    2. The Body Burns Stored Fat for Fuel 142

    3. Fasting Supports Heart Health and Longevity 144

    4. Fasting Reduces Inflammation and Promotes Healing 144

    5. Fasting Improves Mental Clarity 147

    6. Fasting Resets Emotional Patterns 148

    7. Fasting Rebuilds Discipline and Self-Control 149

    8. Fasting Improves Sleep and Rest 152

    9. Fasting Breaks Food Addiction and Cravings 152

    10. Fasting Supports Spiritual Focus Through Physical Alignment 154

    Conclusion: Your Body is a Partner in Your Spiritual Journey 156

Chapter 10: Discipline of Consistency: Making Fasting a Lifestyle, Not an Event 159

    1. Fasting was Designed to be a Rhythm, not a Rare Practice 159

    2. Consistency Builds Spiritual Maturity 161

    3. Weekly Rhythms: The Power of the One-Day Fast 162

    4. Monthly or Quarterly Extended Fasts 164

© 2026 Dr. Thomas L. Driver, Ph.D., DMIN. All Rights Reserved.
Published by TLDM Evangelistic Media Network

5. Daily Rhythms: Intermittent Fasting as
Spiritual Discipline 165

6. Consistency Requires Intentionality 166

7. Overcoming Hindrances to Consistency 167

8. The Power of Long-Term Momentum 169

9. Lifestyle of Fasting Prepares You for
Your Calling 169

10. Consistency Turns Fasting into Joy,
Not a Burden 171

Conclusion: Consistency is the Bridge between
Intention and Transformation 171

Chapter 11: Emotional Journey of Fasting: Navigating Feelings, Struggles, and Spiritual Breakthrough 173

1. Fasting Brings Hidden Emotions to the Surface ... 174

2. Fasting Reveals Emotions We Use Food
to Comfort 175

3. Emotional Sensitivity is Normal in Fasting 176

4. Fasting Helps Heal Past Trauma 178

5. Fasting Helps Break Emotional Bondages 179

6. Fasting Calms Anxiety and Mental Overload 180

7. Fasting Increases Emotional Strength 181

8. How to Navigate Emotional Struggles
During a Fast 181

9. Emotional Healing Leads to Spiritual
Breakthrough 184

© 2026 Dr. Thomas L. Driver, Ph.D., DMIN. All Rights Reserved.
Published by TLDM Evangelistic Media Network

10. Fasting Strengthens Identity and
Confidence in God 185

Conclusion: Fasting Heals the Heart and
Strengthens the Soul 186

Chapter 12: Spiritual Warfare During Fasting:
Understanding the Battle and Walking in Victory 188

   1. Fasting Exposes the Enemy's Resistance 189

   2. Why the Enemy Attacks During Fasting 191

   3. Patterns of Warfare During Fasting 193

   4. Example of Jesus: How to Fight During Fasting .. 196

   5. Word of God is Your Primary Weapon 198

   6. Prayer is the Power that Drives Out Darkness 199

   Use These Forms of Warfare Prayer: 199

   7. Worship Breaks Warfare 199

   8. Role of Angels During Your Fast 200

   9. Walking in Victory During Fasting 201

   10. What to Do When the Warfare Feels Intense 202

   My Reflection: Fasting in Seasons of
   Personal Battle 208

   Conclusion: Fasting Strengthens You for Battle 209

Chapter 13: Rewards of Fasting: What God
Releases Into Your Life 210

   1. God Rewards Those Who Seek Him in Secret 211

   2. Fasting Opens the Door to Revelation 211

   3. Fasting Releases Breakthrough 213

4. Fasting Brings Deliverance and Freedom 213
5. Fasting Increases Spiritual Authority 214
6. Fasting Deepens Intimacy with God 215
7. Fasting Strengthens Character 216
8. Fasting Releases Divine Favor 217
9. Fasting Brings Breakthrough in Prayer 219
10. Fasting Restores Peace, Joy, and Emotional Strength 220
11. Fasting Activates God's Protection 221
12. Fasting Positions You for Purpose and Assignment 222
Conclusion: The Rewards of Fasting are Life-Changing 225

Chapter 14 Role of the Holy Spirit in Fasting: Your Helper, Guide, and Strength 226
1. The Holy Spirit Initiates the Fast 227
2. The Holy Spirit Strengthens You During the Fast . 228
3. The Holy Spirit Deepens Your Prayer Life 229
4. The Holy Spirit Gives Revelation and Understanding 230
5. The Holy Spirit Breaks Bondage and Strongholds 232
6. The Holy Spirit Aligns You with God's Will 233
7. The Holy Spirit Builds the Fruit of the Spirit in You 233

8. The Holy Spirit Protects You from the Enemy's Attacks 235

9. The Holy Spirit Helps You Hear the Voice of God 236

10. The Holy Spirit Sustains You to Finish the Fast 237

11. The Holy Spirit Transforms You from the Inside Out 238

My Reflection: My Life with the Holy Spirit through Fasting 238

Conclusion: The Holy Spirit is the Center of Every Successful Fast 240

Chapter 15: Drawing Closer to God Through Fasting: Deepening Intimacy, Relationship, and Spiritual Sensitivity 243

1. Fasting Positions You to Seek God Wholeheartedly 244

2. Fasting Creates Space for God's Presence 245

3. Fasting Sharpens Your Ability to Hear God's Voice 246

4. Fasting Deepens Your Hunger for God 247

5. Fasting Purifies the Heart 248

6. Fasting Strengthens Your Dependence on God 249

7. Fasting Helps You Recognize God's Movements in Your Life 250

8. Fasting Helps You Fall in Love With God Again .. 251

© 2026 Dr. Thomas L. Driver, Ph.D., DMIN. All Rights Reserved.
Published by TLDM Evangelistic Media Network

9. Fasting Builds a Friendship With God...................253

10. Fasting Aligns Your Heart with God's Will 253

Conclusion: Fasting Draws You Into the
Heart of God 255

Life Set Apart: Embracing Fasting and Prayer as a
Lifestyle of Power, Purpose, and
Intimacy with God 256

11. Fasting Is About Relationship, Not Restriction...257

12. Fasting Strengthens What Matters Most 258

13. Fasting Is the Believer's Secret Place of Power..260

14. Fasting Makes You Spiritually Dangerous..........260

15. Fasting Leads You to Your God-Given
Purpose 261

16. Fasting Cultivates a Life of Discipline
and Holiness 262

17. Fasting Teaches Dependence on the
Holy Spirit 263

18. Fasting Is a Witness of Your Faith 264

19. Fasting Is for Every Christian, Not Just the
"Strong" Ones..265

20. Your Next Step: Make Fasting a Lifestyle 266

A Final Word From My Heart to Yours 267

Chapter 16: Menu Guide 1 The Biblical Daniel Diet
(Daniel 1 & Daniel 10) 269

Biblical Foundation...270

General Principles...270

© 2026 Dr. Thomas L. Driver, Ph.D., DMIN. All Rights Reserved.
Published by TLDM Evangelistic Media Network

Approved Foods 270
Foods To Avoid 273
Sample 10–Day Menu 273
Chapter 17: Healthy Bread and Water Fast 276
Purpose of the Bread and Water Fast 277
Best Breads for This Fast (And Why) 278
Recommended Breads 278
Breads To Avoid 280
How To Make Electrolyte Water
(Safe & Fast-Friendly) 281
Chapter 18: Daily Fasting Schedule
(Applies to All Durations) 283
Morning (Water Only) 283
Midday Meal (Bread + Water) 283
Evening Meal (Bread + Water) 283
Before Bed 284
Chapter 19: Complete Fasting Protocols 285
3-Day Healthy Bread & Water Fast 285
5-Day Healthy Bread and Water Fast 286
7-Day Healthy Bread and Water Fast 287
Chapter 20: Important Safety Guidelines 289
Do NOT attempt this fast if you: 289
How To Break The Fast Safely 290

© 2026 Dr. Thomas L. Driver, Ph.D., DMIN. All Rights Reserved.
Published by TLDM Evangelistic Media Network

Chapter 21: How to Break Your Fast with the Lord's Supper 291

    Step-By-Step Process 292

    What Happens in the Spirit When You Break Your Fast this Way 294

    Why Every Christian Should Do This 294

Chapter 22: My Testimony: How Fasting, Prayer, and Communion Transformed My Life 296

References 302

About the Book..308

About the Author 311

More Books on Prayer by Dr. Thomas L. Driver, PhD, DMIN 312

© 2026 Dr. Thomas L. Driver, Ph.D., DMIN. All Rights Reserved.
Published by TLDM Evangelistic Media Network

Chapter 1: Understanding Fasting: Returning to God with Your Whole Heart

Fasting is a Christian practice involving abstaining from food or pleasures to strengthen spiritual connection, express penitence, or seek guidance. It encourages discipline, humility, and reliance on God.

Throughout history, from the prophets and kings of Israel to the Apostles and early Church believers, fasting has been a meaningful way to deepen intimacy, gain clarity, seek repentance, and build spiritual strength.

Unfortunately, many believers today fast in a more relaxed or inconsistent way, sometimes for reasons that are not quite right. They fast because they believe thoughts of spiritual cleansing will occur if the mind is not fully aligned with God.

Some see it as just an optional ritual, others treat it like a diet plan, and some even avoid it because they don't fully understand its true purpose.

By gaining a deeper understanding of its significance, we can approach fasting with greater meaning and sincerity, allowing us to connect more authentically with its purpose.

But biblical fasting is neither punishment nor performance. It is a call—a divine invitation to return to God with the whole heart. It is a conscious, Spirit-led choice to seek the Lord above comfort, routine, and even physical needs.

Through fasting, we silence distractions, confront our spiritual condition, and acknowledge our dependence on God for every breath and each victory.

This chapter lays the foundation: what fasting is, what it is not, and why it is essential for every believer who desires a deeper walk with Christ.

Fasting is Not About Food— It is About Focus

Many see fasting mainly as giving up food or other things. However, the Word of God reveals that fasting is about whom we turn to.

The physical act of avoiding food makes room for spiritual focus. It interrupts our usual routines so we can intentionally seek God, something we often overlook when life feels easy.

Fasting is not:

- a Christian diet
- a cleansing program
- a hunger strike to persuade God
- a method to impress others
- a way to gain spiritual superiority

Fasting is not a form of self-punishment or emotional manipulation. Instead, it is a grace-filled spiritual discipline intended to foster a deeper relationship with the Lord, helping believers to draw nearer to Him through dedicated devotion and mindfulness.

Scripture explains it clearly:
"I humbled myself with fasting."
—Psalm 35:13, NKJV

"Man shall not live by bread alone, but by every word that proceeds from the mouth of God."
—Matthew 4:4, NKJV

Fasting is a posture of humility, an acknowledgment that we depend on God more than on physical nourishment. Through the temporary weakening of the body, God strengthens the spirit.

By emptying ourselves of natural cravings, we become more receptive to the voice of the Holy Spirit.

Fasting is not merely about denying the body sustenance; it is a profound practice that awakens and nurtures the soul, fostering inner growth and enlightenment.

Call to Return to God

Fasting is regarded as a divine invitation from God to His people, offering a spiritual discipline and a deeper connection with Him. In the Old Testament, the Lord specifically directed Israel on the practice and significance of fasting.

"Consecrate a fast, call a sacred assembly."
—Joel 1:14, NKJV

This was not merely a suggestion; it was a divine summons to repentance, a call for sincere self-reflection, realignment with spiritual principles, and renewal of the heart and mind. The same expectation persists into the New Testament, exemplified in the words of Jesus when He said:

*"**When** you fast…"*
—Matthew 6:16, NKJV

Not *if*. When.

Fasting is not optional for serious believers. It is the rhythm of a **_consecrated life._** It is the bridge between prayer and breakthrough. And it is the spiritual discipline that prepares the heart to hear the voice of God more clearly.

Throughout all seasons of biblical history, fasting has signified moments of transition, repentance, and divine guidance. When God sought to reveal, shift, or revive His people, He frequently called them to fast.

Today, He still calls us.

My Journey into a Lifestyle of Fasting

I developed my understanding of fasting well before I entered ministry, pastoral leadership, or academic study. It started in my childhood at Catholic school. It persisted throughout my military career, including remote assignments, service on ships, deployments, and periods of intense pressure where discipline was essential for survival.

Twenty-seven years in the military taught me the importance of sacrifice, discipline, and perseverance. Those lessons later became the foundation of my faith journey and a discipline of fasting and prayer.

From early in my Christian journey, fasting evolved from an occasional act to a consistent way of life. I adopted a weekly fasting routine, including Sabbath fasts, that revived my spirit and reoriented my focus.

I've spent extended periods fasting—like 10-day fasts where I ate only eggs or vegetables, the Daniel fast at the beginning of each year, and even moments when I completely abstained, relying on God's comforting presence. These experiences have truly enriched my spiritual journey.

Trying the 18:6 intermittent fasting plan—fasting for 18 hours and eating all meals within a 6-hour period—has been unexpectedly great.

Not only have I noticed clearer thinking, improved focus, and increased strength, but my mood and overall well-being have also improved. This has been a highly positive change for both my body and mind!

By fasting and eating clean foods, mainly with single ingredients and not processed or chemically infused, God restored my health, mind, body, and spirit after difficult periods in the wilderness, hardship, and spiritual battles.

Fasting has been essential in my life, enhancing my sermon preparation and problem-solving as a minister, sharpening my focus as a professor and mentor, and providing stability in my roles as husband and leader.

I've found that fasting actually enhances my strength and vitality rather than reducing it. It acts as a great support system, strengthening my body, mind, and spirit for whatever challenges come my way.

Through this practice, I have noticed steady improvements in strength and resilience, along with gradual increases in endurance, mental clarity, and emotional stability.

Fasting has become a key part of my personal growth, significantly boosting my ability to face challenges with more energy and confidence.

Fasting and Prayer: Two Sides of the Same Sword

Fasting without prayer is mainly a physical act, involving abstaining from food and drink. Yet, this practice can act as a gateway to deeper spiritual contemplation.

The hunger felt during fasting often encourages individuals to reflect on their spiritual lives, strengths, and weaknesses. It can inspire a desire for personal growth and a stronger relationship with their faith, motivating them to find meaning and purpose beyond the physical aspect.

Prayer without fasting can lead to distraction and hinder spiritual growth, while combining fasting with sincere prayer is said in Scripture to provide access to divine power and strengthen our connection with God.

Jesus fasted and prayed (see Matthew 4:2, NKJV), while Daniel also fasted to seek greater understanding (see Daniel 1:8, NKJV). Furthermore, members of the early Church fasted and dedicated themselves to serving the Lord (see Acts 13:2, NKJV).

Fasting enhances prayer by shifting the heart from routine habits to a deeper spiritual focus. During fasting, prayers become more focused, worship feels more meaningful, and scripture appears more vivid. What once seemed dull now feels lively, and what once seemed distant now feels near.

When I fasted without a focused prayer time, I felt little spiritual movement. But when I combined my fasting with intentional and focused time in God's presence, something changed.

Old patterns broke, and my priorities were reset. My spirit became more aware of His guidance. Fasting cleared away the noise, and prayer brought me into the quiet place where God speaks.

Fasting is for Every Believer

Many believers hesitate to fast, believing it's a practice only the spiritually "advanced" can undertake. Others feel too weak, busy, or inexperienced to attempt fasting.

However, Scripture encourages all believers, whether new to their faith or walking with God for years, to participate in fasting (Matthew 6:16–18, NKJV).

Fasting is a personal journey that not only strengthens your relationship with God but also encourages spiritual growth and constantly reminds you of His divine presence in every part of your life.

For those just beginning, consider skipping one meal, fasting until noon, or even doing a one-day fast while dedicating time to Scripture and prayer.

© 2026 Dr. Thomas L. Driver, Ph.D., DMIN. All Rights Reserved.
Published by TLDM Evangelistic Media Network

Taking these small, personalized steps can help you establish a meaningful spiritual rhythm and build lasting momentum.

Experienced believers typically deepen their spiritual journey through longer fasts and personal disciplines such as extended prayer, journaling, silence, and worship, making their faith experience more meaningful and tailored.

But the truth remains: Anyone who desires a closer relationship with God can choose to fast.

Fasting is not a measure of spiritual achievement; rather, it stems from a deep spiritual hunger and longing for God's presence, as Scripture emphasizes.

For example, Jesus said in Matthew 6:16–18 (NKJV), *"When you fast, do not look somber as the hypocrites do... but when you fast, anoint your head and wash your face, so that it will not be obvious to others that you are fasting, but only to your Father, who is unseen; and your Father, who sees what is done in secret, will reward you."*

Fasting is a profoundly personal act of devotion that reflects an individual's commitment to their spiritual journey and responds to their inner spiritual hunger.

God compassionately fulfills the desires of those who hunger and thirst for Him, as Jesus assured in Matthew 5:6 (NKJV):

"Blessed are those who hunger and thirst for righteousness, for they shall be satisfied."

This divine promise highlights God's deep compassion and willingness to provide spiritual nourishment to all who earnestly seek Him, ensuring that His loving grace ultimately meets their spiritual needs.

Guarding the Heart: Fasting is not Performance.

Jesus cautioned His disciples against turning fasting into a show of self-righteousness, emphasizing sincerity and personal devotion.

"Do not be like the hypocrites..."—a reminder to reflect on the importance of sincerity and authenticity in our faith, as emphasized in Matthew 6:5–6 (NJKV).

By reflecting on our motives and actions, we can aim to embody genuine humility and integrity in our daily lives, rather than merely seeking outward recognition or approval, echoing the call in James 4:10 (NJKV) to humble ourselves before the Lord.

Fasting is not meant to showcase spirituality. It is a personal act of devotion rooted in sincerity and humility. When fasting is used to seek attention or praise from others, its true spiritual significance diminishes, and its impact weakens.

© 2026 Dr. Thomas L. Driver, Ph.D., DMIN. All Rights Reserved.
Published by TLDM Evangelistic Media Network

The true purpose of fasting is based on sincerity, secrecy, humility, and a pure heart. As highlighted in Scripture, such as Matthew 6:16–18 (NJKV), fasting should be done privately to earn a genuine reward from God.

Absolute fasting is more than merely declaring one's commitment; it involves integrating this practice into every facet of daily life through persistent effort, disciplined routines, and unwavering dedication to spiritual and physical discipline.

This commitment involves incorporating fasting into daily routines, practicing mindfulness, and developing a mindset centered on spiritual growth and self-control.

Fasting as a Way of Life

Fasting goes beyond a single act; it represents a continual way of life. It embodies a rhythm of regularly turning to God with openness, dependence, and surrender. It serves as the believer's declaration.

"Lord, You are my sustenance. You are my strength. You are my source."

When fasting becomes a consistent part of your Christian journey, everything begins to transform, deepening your connection with God and shaping your spiritual growth.

- the mind becomes clearer
- the heart becomes softer

- the spirit becomes stronger
- the will becomes surrendered
- the flesh becomes subdued
- the believer becomes attentive to the Holy Spirit

Fasting goes beyond abstaining; it promotes meaningful physical, mental, and spiritual growth. By giving up certain foods or habits, people can reset their bodies, improve clarity, and better understand themselves.

† It returns us to the heart of worship.

† It anchors us in humility.

† It draws us into God's presence.

It prepares us for good work by providing the essential skills and mindset needed to achieve our purpose and succeed in our endeavors.

Conclusion: Fasting Leads Us Back to God

Understanding the true meaning of fasting is fundamental to the journey presented in the book. Fasting goes beyond merely skipping meals; it is a sincere act of directing your heart toward God with humility and devotion. It serves as the believer's way of expressing:

"Lord, I need You more than anything else."

† Fasting clears the fog.

© 2026 Dr. Thomas L. Driver, Ph.D., DMIN. All Rights Reserved.
Published by TLDM Evangelistic Media Network

† Fasting awakens spiritual hunger.

† Fasting strengthens the soul.

† Fasting draws us into God's presence.

Practicing biblical fasting reconnects us with an essential part of the Christian journey, as shown in Matthew 6:16–18 (NJKV), where Jesus tells us to fast honestly and in private.

This tradition traces back to the ancient rhythms that influenced the prophets (Joel 2:12–14, NJKV), supported the early church (Acts 13:2–3, NJKV), and sustained Jesus Himself (Matthew 4:1–2, NJKV).

Fasting is more than merely a spiritual discipline for Christians; it is a fundamental aspect of our identity and faith.

It embodies our ongoing, profound hunger for God, showcasing our deep spiritual longing and unwavering commitment to seek Him earnestly.

Through fasting, we openly express our deep desire to cultivate a closer, more meaningful relationship with Him. It reaffirms our unwavering commitment to maintaining His presence in our daily lives, strengthening our faith and spiritual connection.

Chapter 2:
The Heart Behind Fasting:
Place Where Transformation Begins

Fasting is a powerful practice, but its true strength lies in the intention behind it. The Bible never treats fasting as just an empty ritual or a simple religious duty; instead, it highlights the heartfelt devotion behind it.

Instead, biblical fasting comes from a heartfelt place—a genuine longing for God, a sincere desire for holiness, a humble spirit, and a yearning for transformation.

When our hearts are aligned with God's purposes, fasting becomes a meaningful and sacred journey toward a closer, more intimate relationship with Him.

This chapter reminds us that when we fast, God's genuine desire isn't just about going through the motions but about truly opening our hearts and sincerely surrendering.

By approaching fasting with openness and commitment, we can truly experience its significance and find deeper fulfillment and meaning along the way.

© 2026 Dr. Thomas L. Driver, Ph.D., DMIN. All Rights Reserved.
Published by TLDM Evangelistic Media Network

True Fasting Begins with the Heart, Not the Stomach

Many people start fasting by thinking about what they can't eat. But biblical fasting isn't about the body; it's about the heart. It begins with desire, repentance, humility, and a longing for God. Traditional rituals may change our daily routines, but heart-led fasting changes our lives.

The Prophet Joel explicitly and succinctly expressed this truth, rendering it accessible to his audience.

"Turn to Me with all your heart, with fasting, with weeping, and with mourning."
—Joel 2:12, NKJV

Notice the order:

1. Turn to Me with your heart
2. Then fast
3. Then let the outward signs follow

Fasting is an expression of a heart already turning toward God. It is the outward proof of inward hunger. When the heart turns first, fasting becomes worship—not performance.

Throughout my fasting journey, I realized that the most meaningful fasts weren't always the longest. Instead, they were the times when my heart was truly broken, humbled, and surrendered to a higher purpose.

When I consciously declared, **"Lord, I desire You more than food, more than comfort, more than my routine,"** a profound change occurred within me.

Fasting evolved from just denying my body to becoming an act of opening my heart to God's transformative power, letting Him reshape my soul from within.

Reward of Sincere Fasting

In the Sermon on the Mount, Jesus addressed fasting with profound clarity. He warned His disciples not to disfigure their faces or broadcast their sacrifice. Instead, He taught them to fast in secret, with sincerity and purity of motives:

"...and your Father who sees in secret will reward you openly."
—Matthew 6:18, NKJV

The reward of fasting does not come from public approval. It comes from the God who sees our hearts.

Sincere fasting produces:
- deeper relationship with God
- renewed spiritual hunger
- clarity of purpose
- strength in temptation
- breakthrough during battles
- greater sensitivity to the Holy Spirit

© 2026 Dr. Thomas L. Driver, Ph.D., DMIN. All Rights Reserved.
Published by TLDM Evangelistic Media Network

- healing in hidden places
- freedom from bondage

When we fast with a sincere heart, we create space for God to reveal Himself in ways we could not access through routine prayer alone.

Fasting is not a currency to buy God's blessing. Fasting is a posture that prepares us to receive what God already desires to give.

Dependence on God, Not Self-Sufficiency

Fasting humbles us by revealing what we lean on. It exposes our dependencies—food, comfort, routine, emotion, entertainment, attention, and even our own strength.

When these external influences are removed, what remains is our true internal yearning for fulfillment. The psalmist expressed this longing beautifully:
"My soul thirsts for God, for the living God."
—Psalm 42:2, NKJV

Fasting turns physical hunger into a sense of spiritual awareness. Every hunger pang serves as a reminder that our soul yearns for something greater, higher, and everlasting.

Every moment of weakness turns into a gentle call inviting us into God's presence. That's why fasting heightens the spirit's sensitivity—it sharpens the soul, making it more alert and open to God's things.

During seasons of fasting, I have often found myself more aware of God's voice than at any other time, as abstaining from certain foods or activities creates a quiet space for reflection and spiritual connection, making His presence and guidance more evident in my life.

† The noise of life quiets.

† The mind simplifies.

† The heart becomes tender.

I learned to pray in weakness and worship in surrender. And each time, God filled the empty places with His strength, peace, and wisdom.

Fasting marks the point at which human effort ceases and divine empowerment takes over, guiding and strengthening individuals beyond their own limitations.

My Personal Journey: Discovering the Heart of Fasting

Fasting has profoundly impacted various aspects of my life, extending beyond my spiritual journey to influence my character, emotions, health, and leadership abilities.

Over the years, I have come to realize that fasting exposes a person's true nature, revealing who they are when the familiar comforts of routine are removed.

It reveals the hidden areas of the heart—impatience, pride, frustration, fear, distraction—and presents them to God for transformation.

Intermittent Fasting: Clarity and Focus

During my intermittent fasting, such as the 18:6 routine, I fast for 18 hours and eat within a 6-hour window. I usually have my first meal after 12 PM and a second around 4:30 PM, finishing by 6 PM, then refrain from eating until noon the following day. I observed that my mind became clearer and I felt more alert.

Prayer felt more meaningful, worship seemed more personal, and scripture became clearer and more inspiring. It's wonderful how these moments bring such a positive boost to my spiritual and mental well-being.

Sabbath Fasts: Rest for the Soul

My weekly 24-hour Sabbath fasts served as vital moments of spiritual recalibration. During these periods, God worked to eliminate the lingering residue of the week—stress, distractions, and pressures—and replaced them with a sense of rest, gratitude, and renewal.

God established the Sabbath fast for man, not the other way around. It is a time to rest the body from work, which, to me, includes refraining from eating.

This principle is *deeply rooted in scripture—Jesus Himself taught, "The Sabbath was made for man, not man for the Sabbath"* (Mark 2:27, NKJV). This means the Sabbath is a gift from God, designed for our benefit, restoration, and connection with Him.

When I observe a Sabbath fast, I honor this divine intention by resting not only from labor but also from food, allowing my body and spirit to recalibrate and draw closer to God.

I take this practice very seriously. It's not a casual or optional tradition for me; it's an act of obedience and reverence. Each week, I set aside this sacred time, fully abstaining from work and meals, trusting that God's design for the Sabbath brings true renewal.

This discipline reflects my commitment to place God's priorities above my own routines. It's a way of surrendering control, acknowledging my dependence on Him, and creating space for His presence to restore my soul.

In doing so, I strive to honor the heart behind the Sabbath as Jesus taught, making it a cornerstone of my spiritual journey.

Extended Fasts: Hunger for God's Voice

During prolonged fasting periods, such as a 10-day fast comprising eggs, vegetables, or bread, I noticed that, more often than not, God communicates with us through the steady, consistent rhythms of life and nature.

These fasts weren't about proving strength; they were about humbly and faithfully positioning myself before God. Each day, the initial physical discomfort gradually gave way to a deeper spiritual awareness.

I remember waking up on the fourth morning feeling especially weak, yet there's an undeniable sense of peace and clarity. It was as if, without my usual comforts and routines, I could hear God's voice more clearly, guiding my thoughts and stirring my heart toward greater surrender.

While fasting, I became aware of some personal tendencies that usually go unnoticed—such as impatience, mild anxiety, and a deep need for security. This experience encouraged me to acknowledge these areas and present them to God for healing and growth.

There were times when hunger felt overwhelming, but that emptiness transformed into an offering—a space for God's presence to fill me with new strength and perspective.

Each meal I skipped became a purposeful act of worship, a silent acknowledgment that my deepest hunger was for God Himself, not just for food.

By the end of the fast, I felt my spirit renewed, my mind clearer, and my heart more tuned to God's voice, ready to embrace whatever He was calling me to next.

Military Heart Transformed by the Spirit

As a retired naval officer, I've found that true strength comes from endurance and discipline. Over the years, fasting has helped me discover an even deeper kind of strength—trust and reliance on God.

While physical discipline enabled me to handle many challenges, it was spiritual discipline that truly equipped me for all that life has presented, making my faith and dependence on God the core of my journey.

Scholar and Pastor Shaped by Consecration

As a professor and educator, fasting has profoundly enhanced my clarity during challenging decision-making and teaching moments. It has sharpened my focus, deepened my insights, and enriched my understanding, enabling me to serve my students more effectively.

Throughout my experiences as both a pastor and an author, fasting has consistently inspired me, offered new insights, strengthened my spiritual resilience, and deepened my understanding of faith and devotion.

These periods of abstinence have led to some of my most impactful sermons, meaningful writing, and personal breakthroughs—moments when I genuinely feel a deep connection to my faith and purpose.

© 2026 Dr. Thomas L. Driver, Ph.D., DMIN. All Rights Reserved.
Published by TLDM Evangelistic Media Network

Fasting has played a key role in my personal growth, helping me progress in my career and deepen my spiritual life by cultivating discipline, self-reflection, and resilience.

By dedicating time to this practice, I have gained greater discipline, clarity, and focus, which have positively influenced my professional pursuits and spiritual understanding.

† Fasting refined my mind.

† Fasting humbled my heart.

† Fasting sharpened my spirit.

† Fasting prepared my calling.

Fasting Reveals What Needs Transformation

Fasting acts as a profound diagnostic tool for the soul, allowing us to uncover and reflect on insights and truths that might otherwise remain concealed.

This spiritual practice encourages deep self-examination, reminding us of 2 Corinthians 13:5, which urges us to evaluate ourselves carefully and sincerely in our faith and inner state.

- hidden fears
- buried emotions
- unhealthy attachments
- spiritual complacency

- ungodly habits
- misplaced priorities
- the places where God desires deeper surrender

And it also awakens:
- perseverance
- spiritual hunger
- compassion
- holiness
- reverence
- greater dependence on the Spirit

Every fast serves as a mirror—reflecting both our true selves and the ongoing work God is doing to shape us into the people He calls us to be.

This process can sometimes be challenging because it forces us to face our dependencies and weaknesses, but it is also a profoundly transformative practice.

Through fasting, God refines, purifies, and realigns our hearts and minds with His divine will, guiding us toward spiritual growth and renewal.

Fasting as Worship: A Living Sacrifice

Fasting goes beyond just refraining from food; it becomes a heartfelt act of worship. When we choose to fast, we are offering our bodies as a gift, aligning our intentions with

Paul's heartfelt encouragement to dedicate ourselves fully to spiritual growth and connection.

> *"Present your bodies a living sacrifice, holy, acceptable to God, which is your reasonable service."*
> —Romans 12:1, NKJV

In Psalm 63, as David wandered through the wilderness, his hunger evolved into a heartfelt cry for God, reflecting his deep yearning and reliance on divine sustenance.

> *"My soul follows close behind You; Your right hand upholds me."*
> —Psalm 63:8, NKJV

True fasting is the echo of that same cry. It is the way believers say, *"Lord, I want You more than my comfort. More than my cravings. More than my schedule. You are my portion and my pursuit."*

When fasting is regarded as an act of worship, it often leads to profound personal transformation, making it an integral part of spiritual growth and self-discovery.

Expectation: Atmosphere of Breakthrough

Fasting without expectation is simply deprivation; it lacks purpose or hope. When we approach fasting with expectation, it transforms into a decisive breakthrough.

© 2026 Dr. Thomas L. Driver, Ph.D., DMIN. All Rights Reserved.
Published by TLDM Evangelistic Media Network

Throughout Scripture, God responded to those who fasted with anticipation—trusting in His deliverance, healing, revelation, wisdom, protection, and renewal.

These acts of faith personalized our connection with God, reminding us that our sincere hopes and trust can unlock His divine intervention in our lives.

Fasting has reliably offered clarity, strength, and guidance when prayer alone was not enough, providing comfort and courage during stressful or uncertain times.

Expectation does not dictate God's actions; rather, it beautifully demonstrates our sincere faith that He will personally encounter us during our quietest, most private moments.

Conclusion:
The Heart Determines the Harvest

The heart is where fasting begins—and where its greatest blessings are released. When believers approach fasting with humility, sincerity, purity, and hunger for God, fasting becomes a sacred encounter with His presence.

The heart behind fasting determines:
- the depth of transformation
- the clarity of revelation
- the power of breakthrough
- the intimacy with God

- the fruit that remains

Fasting, when undertaken with sincere intent, can foster personal transformation by encouraging individuals to live in accordance with the Spirit's influence.

When driven by genuine humility, sincere desire, and openness before God, fasting goes beyond mere ritual or religious duty, becoming a powerful path to profound internal transformation.

Indeed, sincere fasting helps to eliminate distractions and reduce reliance on oneself, enabling us to become more open and attentive to the gentle nudges and guidance of the Holy Spirit.

During these peaceful, surrendering moments, our hearts align with God's will, and His grace beautifully shapes who we are. As a result, our choices, attitudes, and relationships with others reflect the tremendous transformation that only God's Spirit can bring about.

Over time, living guided by the Spirit results in wonderful and lasting changes—such as increased love, wisdom, and courage—that remain with us long after the fast has ended. They beautifully mirror God's ongoing work within our hearts.

Chapter 3:
Fasting in the Old Testament: Divine Pattern for Today

Before Jesus fasted in the wilderness, before the Apostles fasted to hear the Holy Spirit, and before the early Church fasted to appoint leaders, fasting was already woven into the fabric of God's people.

The Old Testament provides a divine blueprint—demonstrating how God responds when His people humble themselves, seek His face, and set aside physical nourishment to pursue His presence.
(see *Joel 2:12–13,* and *Ezra 8:21–23,* NKJV).

These stories are more than mere historical accounts; they act as spiritual examples for believers today. Through Moses, Elijah, Esther, David, and Daniel, we observe the same truth repeated:

When God's people fast, His power is shown.

This chapter explores fasting in the Old Testament, highlighting its significance for spiritual discipline and its relevance to personal commitment today.

Moses: Fasting for Revelation

A notable fast described in Scripture is the 40-day period when Moses abstained from food and drink on Mount Sinai. This time underscores Moses' deep spiritual commitment and dependence on divine power.

Often regarded as a period of preparation and divine encounter, where Moses received the Ten Commandments from God, this fast emphasizes the significance of spiritual discipline and connection with God in biblical tradition.

The Scriptures tell us:

"So he was there with the Lord forty days and forty nights; he neither ate bread nor drank water."
—Exodus 34:28, NKJV

This was not human endurance—it was divine sustaining power. Moses fasted because he was in the presence of God. This fast was a supernatural moment of communion, where the glory of God Himself overshadowed physical needs.

During this sacred period, Moses received the Law—the Commandments that fundamentally shaped Israel's national identity and solidified the covenant between God and His people. Fasting was not the primary focus.

Revelation was the ultimate goal, and fasting served to prepare his spirit, creating a receptive state essential for receiving divine insight.

What Moses Teaches Us

✝ Revelation follows consecration

✝ The presence of God sustains what the flesh cannot

✝ Fasting quiets the world so we can hear heaven

✝ Divine assignments require divine preparation

My Reflection

Like Moses, I have fasted for extended periods—sometimes 10 days or more, even reaching 20 or 25 days—focusing on simple foods and deviating from my usual eating patterns.

These experiences have helped me quiet my spirit, gain new insights, and prepare myself physically and mentally. Stepping away from daily distractions and drawing closer to God has brought moments of clarity and support, much like Moses's preparation on the mountain.

During these times, I felt God sharpening my discernment, guiding me through major decisions in both ministry and business, and preparing my heart for what lies ahead.

Like Moses, who learned through faith and leadership, I realize that sincerely and consistently drawing near to God prompts Him to draw closer to us—often in powerful and transformative ways that significantly shape our destiny and life journey.

Elijah: Fasting for Renewal

After Elijah's dramatic victory over the prophets of Baal, he fell into a state of exhaustion and fear. The very prophet who had once called down fire from the sky was now fleeing for his life, overwhelmed by his circumstances.

Scripture reveals Elijah's breaking point:
"It is enough! Now, Lord, take my life!"
—1 Kings 19:4, NKJV

But instead of rebuking Elijah, God responded with compassion and tenderness, acknowledging Elijah's weariness and emotional distress. He saw how exhausted and overwhelmed Elijah had become after his intense efforts and battles and offered comfort and reassurance rather than criticism.

He sent an angel to feed him and restore his strength—before Elijah began his arduous 40-day journey. This gentle act of care showed God's understanding and mercy during a vulnerable moment.

"Arise and eat, because the journey is too great for you."
—1 Kings 19:7, NKJV

Empowered by this divine sustenance, Elijah journeyed for 40 days and nights, reaching the sacred Mount Horeb, deeply connected to his spiritual journey.

Unlike Moses' stationary fast on the mountain, Elijah went on a traveling fast, moving through wilderness, silence, and solitude. During his journey, he sought spiritual connection not in a fixed place but on the move.

When Elijah arrived at the mountain, he heard God in a gentle whisper—a *"still small voice"* (1 Kings 19:12, NKJV). This moment illustrates that divine guidance is often subtle and personal, beyond external appearances or locations.

What Elijah Teaches Us

- God meets us with grace before He calls us into sacrifice
- Fasting restores strength when the soul is weary
- Breakdowns can become breakthroughs
- Renewal often comes in quietness, not drama

My Reflection

Once, after a prolonged period of preaching, counseling, mentoring, and writing, I experienced severe spiritual and emotional exhaustion. During this time, I turned to fasting as a means of renewal, which helped me regain strength and resilience.

God did not scold me for my weakness; instead, He used fasting to restore clarity, courage, and purpose. Like Elijah, I realized that fasting isn't just a way to prepare for victory but also a way to heal after struggles.

Esther: Fasting for Deliverance

Esther's story reveals fasting as spiritual warfare. When Haman plotted the annihilation of the Jewish people, Esther risked her life to intercede for her nation. But before approaching the king, she issued a call:

"Do not eat or drink for three days, night or day… and so I will go to the king, which is against the law; and if I perish, I perish!"
—Esther 4:16, NKJV

This was not just an individual fast; it was a heartfelt collective fast committed to bringing God's people together in unified prayer, strengthening our community, and deepening our faith.

Fasting empowered Esther with supernatural courage, motivating her to face her fears and act decisively. Consequently, the nation received divine favor, leading to a time of blessing and protection.

At the same time, the enemy's plans were successfully thwarted, effectively preventing their malicious schemes from succeeding and ensuring that their efforts were rendered futile.

What Esther Teaches Us

- Fasting unlocks courage in crisis
- Corporate fasting multiplies spiritual power

- God grants favor to those who humble themselves
- Fasting can shift national destiny

My Reflection

I have faced times when challenges seemed impossible to overcome, including legal disputes, business changes, ministry decisions, and personal trials that tested my faith and resilience.

In these moments, fasting served as a comforting discipline that eased my fears, strengthened my resolve, and helped me reconnect with God's larger purpose.

Esther's story constantly reminds me that fasting is not a passive act; it's a powerful weapon that I can wield in moments of need to seek guidance and divine strength.

David: Fasting for Humility

David was a man after God's own heart, admired for his unwavering faith and devotion, yet he was also deeply familiar with grief and repentance.

During his darkest moments of despair, when remorse and sorrow completely overwhelmed him, he found comfort by expressing his emotions through writing, hoping to find understanding and relief.

"I humbled myself with fasting."
—Psalm 35:13, NKJV

For David, fasting was more than a mere ritual; it was a profound stance and a deeply personal act. He would fast not only during times of sin, grief, or spiritual need but also as a deliberate practice to seek clarity, repentance, and closeness to God.

What David Teaches Us

- Fasting brings humility
- Fasting softens a hard heart
- Fasting aligns motives with God's will
- Leaders should fast to stay grounded.

My Reflection

Military leaders often grapple with pride. In my service, fasting acted as a safeguard against it. During promotions, achievements, and the challenges of leadership, fasting reminded me that my strength and successes were not solely my own—they were gifts from God.

These fasting periods helped me stay humble, open to learning, and surrendering, always keeping my reliance on Him front and center. For example, during one particularly challenging fast, I found myself relying even more on prayer and reflection to navigate difficulties.

Daniel:
Fasting for Wisdom and Revelation

Daniel exemplifies fasting as a lifestyle. His first 10-day fast, avoiding rich foods, gave him supernatural strength and clarity, echoing Jeremiah 29:13's promise that those who seek God will find Him.

For me, the Daniel diet is genuinely more than just a health choice; it's a heartfelt spiritual act that helps me feel more connected with God and deepens my faith and devotion.

It aligns beautifully with 1 Corinthians 10:31 (NJKV), reminding me to do everything to bring glory to Him. Choosing to abstain from certain foods inspires me, just like Daniel's unwavering faith and dedication, even when society pressures us to conform.

Practicing this diet provides me with clarity and wisdom, much like the example set by Daniel. It assists me in developing discipline, staying true to my core values, and remaining receptive to divine guidance, which I believe can lead to greater personal growth and spiritual insight.

Every brief, intense moment significantly heightens my awareness, deepening my connection to God's voice and providing me with renewed strength and clarity to confront any challenges that come my way.

© 2026 Dr. Thomas L. Driver, Ph.D., DMIN. All Rights Reserved.
Published by TLDM Evangelistic Media Network

"Their features appeared better and fatter in flesh…"
—Daniel 1:15, NKJV

Subsequently, his 21-day fast led to an angelic visitation and divine revelation.

"I ate no pleasant food… till three whole weeks were fulfilled."
—Daniel 10:2–3, NKJV

Daniel fasted not only to deepen his spiritual connection but also to seek personal understanding and maintain his faith amidst a pagan culture that constantly challenged and tested his beliefs, pushing him to grow stronger and more devoted in his spiritual journey.

What Daniel Teaches Us

- Fasting produces clarity
- Fasting positions us for revelation
- Fasting cultivates discipline and consistency
- Fasting prepares leaders to stand firm in hostile environments

My Reflection

My annual Daniel-type fasts have been moments of profound revelation. God refined my spiritual listening during those times—decisions became more obvious, distractions eased, and wisdom flowed freely.

© 2026 Dr. Thomas L. Driver, Ph.D., DMIN. All Rights Reserved.
Published by TLDM Evangelistic Media Network

Every year, generally in December, I participate in the Daniel Fast by customizing my menu each time, while still strictly following its core principles and guidelines.

My dietary focus remains on simple, plant-based foods, including fresh fruits, vegetables, whole grains, legumes, and nuts.

Some years, I might incorporate more hearty vegetable stews and brown rice, while other years I emphasize fresh salads, roasted sweet potatoes, or homemade bean soups.

I avoid processed foods, sweeteners, and animal products, and I mainly drink water. This variety makes fasting both meaningful and sustainable, reminding me that fasting isn't just an event but a way of life rooted in dedication and intention, as Daniel showed.

Isaiah: Fasting for Transformation

Isaiah 58 gives the most precise definition of God's desired fast:

> *"Is this not the fast that I have chosen:*
> *To loose the bonds of wickedness…*
> *To undo heavy burdens…*
> *To let the oppressed go free…?"*
> —Isaiah 58:6, NKJV

True fasting profoundly transforms the heart, fostering a deeper sense of compassion, an unwavering commitment to justice, and enhanced spiritual authority. It dismantles both internal struggles and external obstacles, liberating individuals and communities alike. This process creates fertile ground for genuine growth, greater understanding, and a more evolved sense of connection with oneself and others.

What Isaiah Teaches Us

- True fasting is more than abstaining—it is acting
- Fasting produces inner transformation
- Fasting empowers believers to impact their world
- God responds to fasting that aligns with His heart

My Reflection

Reflecting on Isaiah 58, I see that fasting has significantly shaped my spiritual growth. It urges me to view fasting not merely as a ritual, but as a way to foster real change—both within myself and in the lives of others.

Each sincere fast has slowly cultivated a gentle yet impactful change in my heart and outlook. It has heightened my awareness of the daily struggles and hardships others endure, nurturing a stronger sense of empathy.

This realization has motivated me to support those in need actively and to spread hope through both small and meaningful actions, trusting that even simple acts of kindness can have a significant impact.

As Isaiah suggests, fasting inspires me to seek justice, lighten my burdens, and serve as a catalyst for healing within my family, church, and community.

Through fasting, I have observed changes not only in my own heart but also in my family, my church, my ministries, and among those I counsel.

Isaiah's teaching reminds me that true fasting breaks the chains of injustice and lifts burdens, empowering me to make a genuine difference in the lives around me.

My journey has shown that when I fast with God's heart, it not only transforms my inner world but also positively changes the atmosphere of every space I enter, bringing peace, clarity, and purpose.

Conclusion:
Blueprint for Today's Believer

The Old Testament reveals a divine pattern:

- Moses fasted for a revelation
- Elijah fasted for renewal
- Esther fasted for deliverance
- David fasted for humility
- Daniel fasted for wisdom
- Isaiah taught fasting for transformation

View these stories not merely as ancient tales or remnants from the past, but as welcoming calls to delve into deeper truths. They encourage us to consider what truly matters and to forge a stronger bond with a greater sense of meaning and purpose in life.

† Fasting prepares us for a divine encounter.

† Fasting aligns us with God's will.

† Fasting strengthens us for spiritual battle.

† Fasting shapes us into vessels God can use.

As I choose to follow this divine pattern, I trust that the same God who worked so powerfully in the lives of Moses, Elijah, Esther, David, and Daniel will also move in my life today.

It is my conviction that clarity, purpose, and resilience will be provided throughout my journey, offering guidance through both challenges and successes.

I trust that divine presence is with me in both success and difficulty, inspired by examples like Esther, David, and Daniel. I believe guidance will come when needed.

With every step, I discover strength and hope through His presence. During tough times, I am reminded that I am not alone; He offers wisdom and perseverance.

Fasting and prayer help me align with His will and become who I am meant to be. This assurance brings peace and encourages a deeper relationship, as each challenge shows His faithfulness and each blessing confirms His love.

© 2026 Dr. Thomas L. Driver, Ph.D., DMIN. All Rights Reserved.
Published by TLDM Evangelistic Media Network

Chapter 4:
Fasting in the New Testament: Lifestyle Modeled by Christ and the Early Church

If the Old Testament lays the foundation of fasting, the New Testament elevates it to a way of life. Jesus did not abolish fasting; He embraced it.

The Apostles did not neglect fasting—they practiced it consistently. And the early Church did not see fasting as optional; it was crucial to their walk with God, their decision-making, and their spiritual power.

My ministry practices New Testament fasting because it symbolizes a deeper, more intentional, and relational way of seeking God, emphasizing a sincere devotion and a personal connection with Him.

Unlike Old Testament fasting, which often focused on national rituals or responses to specific crises, New Testament fasting is a personal discipline rooted in devotion to Christ and empowered by the Holy Spirit.

Jesus Himself exemplified this lifestyle—He fasted not out of obligation but as a means of preparation, consecration, and spiritual alignment before starting His ministry.

The Apostles and early Church continued this practice, viewing fasting as essential for decision-making, spiritual strength, and a closer relationship with God.

By embracing New Testament fasting, our ministry follows the example set by Jesus and the early believers, seeking spiritual renewal, clarity, and a deeper connection with God's purpose for our lives.

This chapter beautifully explores the importance of fasting in the lives of Jesus, the Apostles, and the early Church. It shows how their dedication and spiritual practices can inspire and guide us today, shaping our own spiritual routines and devotion.

Jesus: Fasting Before Ministry

Before delivering sermons, performing miracles, calling disciples, or facing the cross, Jesus fasted. According to Scripture (Matthew 4 & Luke 4), this practice was not just a ritual; rather, it showed deliberate devotion and preparation.

Jesus fasted by choice, seeking to enhance his relationship with God and to gain clarity, strength, and direction for the significant responsibilities that lay ahead.

When I reflect on this, it challenges me to consider my own approach to essential moments in life: do I pause to seek God's direction and align my heart with His purpose, just as Jesus did?

Fasting can serve as a powerful means for spiritual renewal and preparation. Inspired by Jesus' example, I set aside time for prayer and fasting when making important decisions or seeking a deeper connection with God, trusting that intentional devotion leads to meaningful encounters.

"Then Jesus was led up by the Spirit into the wilderness to be tempted by the devil. And when He had fasted forty days and forty nights…"
—Matthew 4:1–2, NKJV

This was not a ritual fast.

It was a Spirit-led fast.

A consecration fast.

A preparation fast.

Jesus fasted not to become the Son of God, but to reveal His divine identity and close relationship with the Father, affirming His mission and nature. This act of fasting served as a powerful testament to His spiritual authority and connection, highlighting the depth of His commitment to fulfilling His divine purpose.

The wilderness was never intended as a place of punishment; instead, it served as a vital space for preparation. In the face of temptation, Jesus drew upon the Scriptures, demonstrating His deep connection to divine truth.

Through reliance on spiritual strength, He resisted the enemy's assaults. Emerging from this trial, Jesus carried with Him newfound power, embodying perseverance and faith that inspire us all.

"Then Jesus returned in the power of the Spirit…"
—Luke 4:14, NKJV

† He entered ministry after He fasted.

† He taught with authority after He fasted.

† He performed miracles after He fasted.

† He announced His mission after fasting.

What Jesus Teaches Us

- Fasting is preparation for a purpose
- Fasting sharpens spiritual discernment
- Fasting strengthens believers for spiritual warfare
- Fasting positions us to walk in spiritual authority

My Reflection

Just as Jesus approached each critical moment in His ministry with purposeful fasting, I've found that intentionally setting aside time to fast has been a meaningful part of every significant milestone in my own journey.

Before starting new initiatives—whether it's writing, leading ministries, making decisions for TLDM Evangelistic Media Network, or mentoring doctoral students—I dedicate myself through fasting, drawing on my experience in evangelistic outreach.

This isn't just a ritual; it's a way to release the old, prepare my heart for what's ahead, and seek God's guidance with renewed focus. Fasting has become a spiritual discipline that enhances my ability to recognize God's guidance.

It's the pause that gets me ready to hear His voice and ensures that each new venture is rooted in His purpose, not merely my own plans.

Engaging in fasting allows me to align my ministry objectives with God's will and prepares me to approach new opportunities with resolve and confidence. This practice has consistently facilitated clarity of vision and enhanced my ability to respond effectively, resulting in purposeful advancement within my ministry work.

© 2026 Dr. Thomas L. Driver, Ph.D., DMIN. All Rights Reserved.
Published by TLDM Evangelistic Media Network

Jesus' Teaching on Fasting: "When You Fast..."

In Matthew 6:16–18 (NKJV), Jesus provides a clear and conviction-driven teaching on fasting. He focuses on the attitude and motives behind fasting, stressing that it should not be done for outward appearances or to impress others.

Instead, Jesus urges believers to fast privately and sincerely, emphasizing a personal relationship with God. By saying, "When you fast," He suggests that fasting is a normal and expected part of the spiritual life, not just an optional practice.

Jesus teaches that fasting should be practiced with humility and sincerity, emphasizing that it is not meant to garner public praise or recognition. Instead, God values and rewards authentic devotion that is performed in secret, reflecting a pure and honest heart.

*"**When** you fast..."*

—not *if*, but *when*

"Do not be like the hypocrites..."

—Fasting is not for display

"Your Father... will reward you openly."

—Fasting done God's way has God's reward.

© 2026 Dr. Thomas L. Driver, Ph.D., DMIN. All Rights Reserved.
Published by TLDM Evangelistic Media Network

Jesus presented fasting as a personal choice, not a strict requirement. In Matthew 6:16–18, He refers to fasting as a typical spiritual practice for strengthening one's connection with God and aligning with His will.

The heart of Jesus' teaching is simple:

Fasting is an act of devotion that God honors.

The Disciples: A Life Shaped by Fasting

John's followers regularly followed strict fasting routines. When asked why His disciples did not fast, Jesus used the opportunity to explain the real reason behind this difference.

"The days will come when the Bridegroom will be taken away from them, and then they will fast."
—Matthew 9:15, NKJV

Jesus was saying:
After my ascension, my followers will observe fasting as a natural expression of their deep longing for me and their reliance on the Spirit, demonstrating their devotion and spiritual dependence.

The Early Church: Fasting for Direction and Assignment

In Acts, fasting played a vital role for the early Church, especially during key decisions and times of uncertainty, as believers relied on God for guidance.

For example, in Acts 13:2 (NKJV), believers fasted and ministered to the Lord, creating an atmosphere in which the Holy Spirit spoke clearly, guiding them to set apart Paul and Barnabas for their missionary work.

Likewise, Acts 14:23 (NKJV) describes leaders praying and fasting as they appointed elders in every church, showing how much they valued aligning with God's will rather than relying solely on human judgment.

These instances emphasize that fasting was seen not just as a ritual, but as an essential way to connect with God, deepen spiritual awareness, and make critical decisions with divine guidance.

1. Fasting While Ministering to the Lord

"As they ministered to the Lord and fasted, the Holy Spirit said..."
—Acts 13:2, NKJV

This verse powerfully demonstrates the close connection between worship, fasting, and hearing from God. The believers weren't fasting to earn a blessing or to persuade God to act in their favor; instead, their fasting was an act of devotion, a way to serve directly before the Lord.

Within that sacred atmosphere, their hearts were profoundly attuned to God's voice, and the Holy Spirit provided unmistakable guidance.

I see fasting isn't just about denying myself food or comfort—it's about creating intentional space to focus on God, honor Him, and seek His presence.

When I choose to fast and worship, I'm not just looking for answers; I'm seeking intimacy with the Lord. In these moments of genuine devotion, God's guidance becomes clear, just as it did for the early church.

Ministering to God through fasting invites His Spirit to speak, lead, and shape my journey in ways I might otherwise miss.

This is powerful.

They were not fasting to get something from God.

They were fasting to minister to Him.

In this atmosphere of sincere worship and devoted fasting, the early believers positioned themselves to truly hear from God. Their hearts were entirely focused on honoring and seeking Him, free from distractions and personal agendas.

In this sacred setting, God chose to reveal His specific plan by directly instructing the Church to set apart Paul and Barnabas for a special apostolic mission, highlighting the divine purpose behind their commissioning.

This pivotal moment emphasizes that when believers earnestly seek God through worship and fasting, they open themselves to receiving clear and purposeful guidance from the Holy Spirit.

The act of fasting didn't manipulate God; instead, it reflected a posture of humility and readiness to embrace His will, leading to a defining assignment that would shape the early Church's future.

2. Fasting for Leadership and Appointments

"So when they had appointed elders in every church, and prayed with fasting..."
—Acts 14:23, NKJV

Leadership decisions were not made casually; fasting served as a spiritual discipline to ensure proper alignment with God's divine will, guiding leaders to make thoughtful and deliberate choices.

This is a crucial principle for pastors, business leaders, ministry teams, and families today. Personally, I've seen how fasting and intentional devotion have changed the way I handle leadership and decision-making.

Fasting has consistently helped me find greater clarity and inner peace, especially when I am faced with making important decisions for my congregation, organization, or family. It enables me to approach these choices with a calmer mind and a more focused perspective.

The early Church regarded fasting as a crucial spiritual discipline that facilitated a deeper connection with God. This practice, rooted in their tradition, continues to hold significant meaning in contemporary faith.

Fasting provides pastors with spiritual insight for wise leadership. Business leaders benefit from seeking guidance before making decisions to align with their values.

Ministry teams foster unity and focus on shared goals by fasting together. Families also find strength through fasting and prayer during challenges.

Fasting serves as a purposeful discipline that encourages humility, increases spiritual awareness, and facilitates openness to receiving divine guidance.

Fasting reminds me that leadership is about serving God and others, not personal ambition. Following the early church's example, we pause and seek guidance, allowing God to shape our decisions beyond our own understanding.

What the Early Church Teaches Us

- Fasting sharpens spiritual sensitivity
- Fasting unlocks prophetic direction
- Fasting prepares leaders for service
- Fasting creates space to hear the Spirit clearly

My Reflection

In my role as both pastor and leader, I rarely make important decisions without first fasting. Whether it's choosing team members, planning for ministry growth, drafting manuscripts, or guiding organizations, fasting has consistently directed me.

Whenever I've faced uncertainty, God has provided direction; during daunting challenges, God has offered peace. The early Church's actions showed me that fasting serves not only a spiritual purpose but is also a strategic practice.

Paul: Fasting as a Lifestyle of Consecration

Paul's ministry was marked by fasting. In 2 Corinthians 6:4–5 (NKJV), he describes being *"in fasting"* frequently, and fasting shaped his endurance, his preaching, and his spiritual authority. His revelation came not from intellect alone but through consecration.

Paul's fasts were not ceremonial; they were relational. They flowed from his love for God, his dependence on Christ, and his commitment to serving the Church.

What Paul Teaches Us

- Fasting sustains spiritual strength
- Fasting fuels revelation
- Fasting enlarges spiritual capacity

© 2026 Dr. Thomas L. Driver, Ph.D., DMIN. All Rights Reserved.
Published by TLDM Evangelistic Media Network

- Fasting keeps believers humble and focused

Paul's example speaks to everyone called to teach, preach, influence, lead, or guide others spiritually because his life demonstrates that effective spiritual leadership is rooted in personal consecration and dependence on God.

Through fasting, Paul consistently sought God's guidance and strength, modeling a lifestyle in which spiritual practices are not merely rituals but integral to sustaining spiritual authority, clarity, and humility.

His approach shows that true influence and leadership in ministry don't come only from human effort or intelligence, but from a deep, ongoing relationship with God, built through dedicated times of fasting, prayer, and reliance on the Holy Spirit.

This motivates every spiritual leader to focus on these disciplines, understanding that they are vital for gaining revelation, staying humble, and serving others with wisdom and strength.

The New Testament Pattern: Fasting + Prayer + Holy Spirit

In the New Testament, fasting is never practiced alone. It is always accompanied by prayer and led by the Holy Spirit. It forms a threefold cord:
- fasting weakens the flesh and deepens my spiritual hunger;

- prayer draws me closer to God's heart and helps me align my desires with His will; and
- The Holy Spirit provides direction, revelation, and empowerment.

Whenever I intentionally practice these three habits—fasting, praying earnestly, and seeking the Holy Spirit's guidance—I find myself feeling a wonderful sense of clarity and strength guiding my spiritual journey.

This pattern isn't just a biblical principle; I've seen it in my own life. There were times when fasting alone felt like not enough, and prayer on its own didn't always bring the breakthrough I wanted. But when I combined all three, it consistently strengthened my body, sharpened my mind, and renewed my soul.

Fasting deepened my sensitivity to God's voice, allowing me to recognize His guidance better. Prayer became a vital practice that helped me listen attentively and respond thoughtfully.

The Holy Spirit's empowerment enabled me to move forward with renewed confidence and purpose, trusting in His strength to sustain me along the way.

This threefold cord is vital for believers, sustaining spiritual growth and providing practical ways to strengthen their relationship with God as they navigate life's challenges.

1. Fasting

Weakening the flesh and increasing spiritual hunger refers to fasting's intentional setting aside of physical comforts and desires, such as food, to focus more deeply on spiritual matters.

By intentionally denying the body its usual cravings, a believer actively acknowledges their reliance on God rather than on fleeting worldly satisfactions, fostering a deeper spiritual connection.

This act of self-discipline helps silence distractions and creates space for a greater awareness of spiritual needs. As physical hunger increases, so does the longing for God's presence and guidance, intensifying the believer's desire for spiritual fulfillment over material comfort.

This process not only humbles the individual but also awakens a deeper thirst for divine revelation, fostering a closer intimacy with God and inspiring a renewed, passionate sense of purpose in their ongoing spiritual journey, encouraging growth and transformation.

2. Prayer

Aligns the believer with God's heart.

To align with God's heart means that, through prayer, a believer intentionally seeks to understand and embrace God's desires, values, and will above their own. Instead of simply presenting personal requests or concerns, prayer becomes a time of listening, surrender, and transformation.

As the believer opens up to God, their motivations and attitudes begin to shift—selfish ambitions fade, and a sincere desire to please God emerges.

This alignment cultivates greater humility, compassion, and discernment, helping the believer handle life's challenges in ways that reflect Christ's love and wisdom.

Ultimately, being in sync with God's heart leads to a deeper relationship with Him, where faith deepens, and life is guided by divine purpose.

3. The Holy Spirit

The Holy Spirit gives direction, revelation, and empowerment by actively guiding believers in their daily lives, illuminating God's will, and providing the strength needed to fulfill His purposes.

When we are attentive to the Holy Spirit, He brings clarity to our decisions, reveals truths that we might otherwise miss, and equips us to overcome challenges with supernatural wisdom and courage.

This is an ongoing partnership in which the Spirit continually guides us, clarifies Scripture, convicts us when needed, and motivates actions aligned with God's will.

This pattern—fasting, prayer, and dependence on the Holy Spirit—remains essential for believers today because it offers a balanced approach to spiritual growth and intimacy with God. In a world filled with distractions and competing voices, these disciplines help us tune out the noise and tune in to God's direction.

By deliberately weakening the flesh via fasting, aligning our hearts with God through prayer, and embracing the Holy Spirit's empowering presence, believers are prepared for continuous transformation and confident faith.

This three-part practice is more than tradition; it is a crucial source of strength, clarity, and spiritual vitality for those seeking a closer relationship with God.

My Reflection

Through years of fasting and prayer as part of my spiritual journey, I have come to a deeper understanding of how intricately these two practices are interconnected.

When I fast without praying, I feel like something is missing, and when I pray without fasting, I sometimes miss out on the breakthrough I want. It's only when I combine both that I truly experience God's transformative power in my life.

Whenever I fast with hope, pray sincerely, and listen attentively for the Holy Spirit's guidance, I am grateful for experiencing God's powerful and life-changing presence.

© 2026 Dr. Thomas L. Driver, Ph.D., DMIN. All Rights Reserved.
Published by TLDM Evangelistic Media Network

He strengthens my body, clears my mind, and refreshes my soul in wonderful ways that enliven every aspect of my being.

Why New Testament Fasting Matters Today

Some argue that fasting is unnecessary under grace. But this misunderstands both Scripture and the nature of grace itself. Grace empowers spiritual discipline, but it does not remove it.

Believers fast today because:
- We desire to walk as Jesus walked
- The Spirit leads us into deeper **consecration**
- Our world is full of distractions
- Our flesh resists the things of God
- We need clarity, power, and discernment
- Spiritual warfare is real
- Leadership requires spiritual stamina
- Revival begins with hunger

Fasting remains important because our reliance on God is equally essential. In a world filled with countless distractions and temptations that draw our attention away from spiritual priorities, fasting serves as a tangible way to humble ourselves and acknowledge our dependence on God's strength and guidance.

© 2026 Dr. Thomas L. Driver, Ph.D., DMIN. All Rights Reserved.
Published by TLDM Evangelistic Media Network

By intentionally forgoing physical comforts, we open ourselves to hearing God's voice, seeking His guidance, and aligning our hearts with His plans.

Fasting calms the distractions of our flesh and the world, enabling us to discern God's direction better and deepen our relationship with Him.

During seasons when we seek clarity, power, and spiritual breakthrough, fasting serves as a strong discipline that strengthens our trust in God and reminds us that proper nourishment comes from Him alone.

Just as Jesus and the early Church depended on fasting to prepare for ministry, make crucial decisions, and withstand spiritual battles, believers today also fast to foster a posture of humility, hunger, and faith in God's ongoing work in their lives.

Conclusion:
Fasting is the New Testament Lifestyle

From Jesus' journeying in the wilderness to the Apostles' missions, and onward to the early Church's worship and decision-making, fasting is a heartfelt thread running through every significant moment in the New Testament.

It lovingly prepared Jesus for His ministry, gently empowered the Apostles, guided the early Church with care, and played a key role in spreading the gospel.

The message is unmistakable: Fasting is not optional for the believer who desires spiritual power, clarity, and purpose. Instead, it is an essential spiritual discipline woven throughout the New Testament and the life of the early church.

Just as Jesus and the Apostles relied on fasting to prepare for ministry, seek God's will, and overcome spiritual opposition, believers today are called to embrace fasting as a vital practice.

It prepares us to gain guidance, strength, and insight from God—essential qualities for strong leadership and success. Fasting humbles us, refocuses our priorities, and opens our hearts to deeper intimacy with God.

In a world filled with distractions and challenges, those who earnestly seek to walk in God's power and fulfill His purpose will find that fasting is not merely a suggestion; it is a foundational way to align ourselves with God's plans and experience transformative spiritual growth.

The Old Testament presents a pattern—a framework for seeking God through intentional practices like fasting and prayer. The New Testament, however, advances this idea by illustrating a way of life to be lived daily and wholeheartedly.

When I choose to follow the example set by Jesus and the early Church, I am not just adhering to tradition; I am adopting a way of living that can give me the same clarity, courage, and spiritual authority they experienced.

Personally, this means that each time I set aside distractions and intentionally seek God, I am actively aligning myself with a rich legacy of faith that extends back through history, connecting with the wisdom and devotion of ancient prophets and reaching forward to the teachings of the Apostles.

Their stories serve as a blueprint for my own spiritual journey. By embracing their practices—especially fasting—I open myself to God's guidance and strength in my daily decisions. The clarity they experienced is available to me when I listen for God's voice.

The courage they showed in facing obstacles can fill my heart when I trust His leading. And the spiritual authority they carried is something I can also walk in as I surrender my plans and desires to Him.

In a world that constantly demands my attention and often pulls me away from what matters most, choosing this lifestyle is a truly transformative decision.

It is not merely about imitating the ways of the past; it is about actively experiencing God's power and presence here and now, embracing His guidance and strength in every moment.

© 2026 Dr. Thomas L. Driver, Ph.D., DMIN. All Rights Reserved.
Published by TLDM Evangelistic Media Network

By following Christ's example and the rhythms of the early church, I can cultivate a life marked by a genuine hunger for God, a deeper intimacy with Him, and a bold, unwavering faith—qualities that are vital for living a purposeful life filled with meaning and making a lasting impact today.

© 2026 Dr. Thomas L. Driver, Ph.D., DMIN. All Rights Reserved.
Published by TLDM Evangelistic Media Network

Chapter 5:
Types of Biblical and Practical Fasts:
Understanding the Paths God Uses to Transform Us

Fasting is not a one-size-fits-all practice. Throughout Scripture, we observe various types of fasts—each serving a unique purpose, rhythm, and spiritual influence—highlighting the diversity and richness of this spiritual discipline.

God never intended fasting to become legalistic or inflexible. Instead, He offers different ways for believers to connect with Him, tailored to other seasons, capacities, and spiritual needs.

In this chapter, we examine the main types of biblical fasts and the practical fasts believers practice today. Whether you're new to fasting or experienced in consecration, you'll find pathways that match your physical ability, spiritual hunger, and personal calling.

1. Complete Fast (Water-Only)

A complete fast involves abstaining from all solid foods and only drinking water. Throughout biblical history, both Moses and Elijah are described as having undergone extraordinary, complete fasts directly empowered and guided by God, emphasizing the spiritual importance and supernatural aspect of these fasts.

Moses: *"He neither ate bread nor drank water."*
—Exodus 34:28, NKJV

Elijah: *"He went in the strength of that food forty days and forty nights."*
—1 Kings 19:8, NKJV

Such occasions are truly extraordinary, occurring rarely and driven by spiritual inspiration rather than personal planning or effort. When individuals feel truly guided by the Holy Spirit, they may choose to undertake a full water-only fast for short periods as a form of spiritual discipline or devotion.

Purpose and Benefits

- Deep cleansing of the soul
- Heightened spiritual sensitivity
- Increased dependence on God
- Powerful breakthrough in seasons of need

My Reflection

During my water-only fasts, I experienced profound healing that touched both my body and my spirit. Physically, abstaining from food allowed my body to undergo a deep cleanse, flushing out toxins and resetting my system.

This process left me feeling lighter and more refreshed, helping restore a sense of overall well-being. Emotionally, the fast brought a rapid emptying of distractions and burdens, making room for renewed energy and focus.

Spiritually, these periods of fasting heightened my sensitivity to God's presence. With my usual routines and comforts stripped away, I became more dependent on God for strength and clarity.

This reliance on divine guidance resulted in profound spiritual breakthroughs, enhancing my ability to hear God's voice more clearly and gain clearer direction for my life.

The fasts were challenging, requiring immense discipline and perseverance, but their impact was undeniable—they provided deep soul cleansing, renewing my spirit and fostering a profound sense of spiritual renewal.

These moments of fasting also strengthened my faith, reaffirming my trust in God's plan for me, and leaving me feeling renewed, more in tune with God's purpose for my life, and spiritually uplifted.

© 2026 Dr. Thomas L. Driver, Ph.D., DMIN. All Rights Reserved.
Published by TLDM Evangelistic Media Network

2. Absolute Fast (No Food or Water)
(Use only under the clear leading of the Holy Spirit and Medical Provider)

Esther called her people to hold a complete fast, abstaining from both food and water for a designated period, often during urgent and critical situations to seek guidance or favor.

According to the biblical story, Esther urged her community to refrain from eating or drinking for three days and nights to seek divine help during a crisis (Esther 4:16, NKJV). This kind of fast is very rigorous and should only be undertaken with clear spiritual guidance, as it is physically demanding.

Spiritually, an absolute fast is believed to enhance one's dependence on God and heighten sensitivity to His presence. Removing every comfort, participants often experience deep soul cleansing, powerful breakthroughs, and renewed clarity.

The fast can lead to urgent deliverance, crisis intervention, and extraordinary spiritual realignment, marking pivotal moments in one's destiny, often serving as a catalyst for profound personal transformation and deeper understanding of one's purpose.

By abstaining from all physical sustenance, individuals not only lessen their dependence on bodily needs but also create space to strengthen their reliance on spiritual strength.

This practice often results in a deeper connection with God and a clearer, more focused sense of purpose, as the soul is nourished through spiritual discipline.

"Do not eat or drink for three days, night or day."
—Esther 4:16, NKJV

Paul fasted without food or water after encountering Christ:
"He was three days without sight, and neither ate nor drank."
—Acts 9:9, NKJV

This type of fast is short, urgent, and undertaken only by divine direction. It is not recommended for extended periods. The absolute fast involves abstaining from both food and water, as seen in the biblical accounts of Esther and Paul.

Because this rapid fasting imposes considerable physical strain, it is reserved for crises or when there's a strong, unmistakable sense that God is guiding the individual to undertake it. These fasts are intended for situations requiring urgent divine intervention, breakthrough, or spiritual renewal.

Attempting an absolute fast without clear spiritual guidance or for too long can be dangerous to one's health, so it should always be approached with caution and reverence, ensuring that the duration does not exceed what the body can safely tolerate.

This underscores the importance of listening closely to God's leading and not engaging in this type of fast simply out of routine or personal desire, but only when vital and for a brief, focused period.

Purpose and Benefits

- Crisis intervention
- Urgent deliverance
- Extraordinary spiritual alignment
- Turning points in destiny

My Reflection

I tend to reserve absolute fasts for truly critical moments—times when something significant is on the line and I feel God's strong conviction in my heart. Even just a one-day absolute fast has often brought me clarity, a sense of alignment, and breakthrough.

To clarify, I do not participate in casual or routine fasts. Instead, I consider this intense form of fasting only in urgent situations—when there is a critical need for divine intervention or guidance.

Such moments often occur when situations seem particularly urgent or during significant transitions. In these times, I feel a clear motivation to fast, seeking guidance and strength through reflection and spiritual discipline.

This decision is always made after thorough prayer and deep spiritual reflection, ensuring that it aligns with divine guidance and genuinely represents the best course of action.

During an absolute fast, I abstain from both food and water, following the examples found in the Bible, such as Esther and Paul. I recognize that this type of fasting puts considerable physical strain on the body and should not be extended beyond what is safe.

Still, dedicating just one day to an absolute fast has significantly impacted my spiritual journey. I experience a deep sense of clarity where confusion gives way to understanding, and my decisions become more aligned with God's will.

Breakthroughs occur, and obstacles that previously appeared insurmountable are eventually overcome. These experiences inspire me with a renewed sense of purpose and a clearer sense of direction, fueling my motivation to keep moving forward.

I approach absolute fasts with reverence, caution, and trust in God's guidance. They are more about faithful response during crises or moments of great need than about personal achievement or discipline. I believe that God will provide the insight, strength, and transformation necessary for the situation.

3. Partial Fast (Restricted Diet) Including the Daniel Fast

This statement highlights that among various types of biblical fasting, the partial fast—often referred to as the Daniel fast—tends to be the most popular and the easiest to keep up over time.

In the Bible, Daniel's experience serves as the primary example of this type of fast. During his fast, Daniel avoided rich foods, meat, and wine, opting instead for simple foods like fruits, vegetables, nuts, and seeds, along with water.

This fasting method is considered sustainable as it does not require complete abstention from food or beverages, making it suitable for extended periods and accessible to a broader range of individuals.

The Daniel Fast is a spiritual practice aimed at fostering greater spiritual clarity, enhancing self-discipline, initiating renewal, and promoting physical wellness.

By following this fast, individuals can support their ongoing spiritual development, deepen their faith, and experience a holistic sense of well-being that encompasses both body and soul.

> "I ate no pleasant food, no meat or wine…nor did I anoint myself at all, till three whole weeks were fulfilled."
> —Daniel 10:3, NKJV

The Daniel Fast generally involves consuming fruits, vegetables, nuts, seeds, and water, while deliberately avoiding meat, sugars, and processed foods to promote spiritual reflection and physical health.

Purpose and Benefits

- Sustained clarity over time
- Spiritual renewal
- Physical cleansing and health benefits
- Training the body in holiness

My Reflection

The Daniel fast plays an essential role in my spiritual growth, offering insight, renewal, and discipline during my annual practice. It has also influenced my writing, ministry, and health.

Each year, as I dedicate myself to this intentional period of fasting, I observe a significant improvement in my ability to hear God's voice clearly and to experience His guidance in fresh and meaningful ways that deepen my faith and understanding.

The practice of abstaining from rich foods, meats, and processed items enhances my spiritual sensitivity, helping me to focus more deeply on prayer and reflection. The simplicity of the diet not only detoxifies my body but also quiets everyday distractions, fostering a stronger sense of peace and clarity.

Through these seasons of fasting, I've seen how spiritual renewal can translate into tangible changes in my day-to-day walk. My writing becomes more inspired, with fresh insight and direction for the messages I share.

In ministry, I have more compassion, patience, and understanding for those I serve. Fasting also boosts my energy, benefits my health, and highlights the value of holistic well-being in spiritual growth.

Overall, the Daniel fast serves as a foundation for my spiritual journey, setting the tone for the year ahead and strengthening habits of self-control and devotion.

The benefits, including spiritual insight, inner cleansing, discipline, and health, extend beyond fasting and significantly impact my life.

4. The One-Meal or Half-Day Fast

This is one of the most straightforward methods for initiating fasting. Practitioners either refrain from a single meal or abstain from all food intake until a specific time, such as noon or 3 p.m.

Purpose and Benefits

- Helps beginners build spiritual discipline
- Teaches the body to yield to the spirit
- Makes fasting accessible for busy individuals

- Creates daily momentum in prayer

This rhythm is especially advantageous for individuals who are just starting to fast again or are in the process of establishing a regular, ongoing spiritual practice, helping to create a steady foundation for their spiritual journey.

5. The 24-Hour Fast or Sabbath Fast

This practice requires abstaining from all food for a full day, typically from dinner the night before until dinner the following evening, or from sunrise to sunrise the next day.

It is considered one of the most spiritually significant disciplines a believer can undertake, especially when practiced weekly, fostering deeper devotion and self-discipline.

Purpose and Benefits

- Weekly spiritual cleansing
- Resets the mind and spirit
- Cultivates humility
- Builds spiritual stamina

My Reflection

My weekly Sabbath fast remains one of the most meaningful spiritual rhythms in my life. Each week, it refreshes my spirit, sharpens my discernment, and draws me into worship. This weekly discipline has taught me consistency, humility, and dependence on God's presence.

6. Intermittent Fasting (or Similar Patterns)

(A practical modern fast with deeply spiritual benefits)

Intermittent fasting has become popular for health reasons, but it also carries profound spiritual value when paired with prayer. This practice offers a variety of benefits for both body and spirit.

Understanding 18:6 and 16:8 Intermittent Fasting

18:6 fasting and 16:8 fasting are two common patterns of intermittent fasting, a dietary approach that alternates periods of eating and fasting to promote health benefits. The numbers in each pattern refer to the hours spent fasting and the hours during which food is consumed each day:

For example, in 16:8 fasting, individuals fast for 16 hours and eat within an 8-hour window, whereas in 18:6 fasting, the fasting period lasts 18 hours and the eating window is 6 hours.

- 18:6 Fasting: You fast for 18 hours and eat all your meals within a 6-hour window. For example, you might eat between 12:00 PM and 6:00 PM, then abstain from food from 6:00 PM until noon the next day.
- 16:8 Fasting: You fast for 16 hours and eat within an 8-hour window. This could mean eating from 10:00

AM to 6:00 PM and fasting from 6:00 PM until 10:00 AM the next morning.

Both methods encourage physical cleansing, weight management, and improved energy, while also providing daily opportunities for spiritual reflection, prayer, and mindfulness.

Limiting eating to a set window can reduce cravings, boost discipline, and enhance mental clarity. This method can help you gain better control over your eating habits and increase your overall focus and cognitive function.

Spiritually, this routine can deepen your sense of dependence on God and create regular moments for worship and prayer, aligning with the benefits described in your context.

Over time, 18:6 and 16:8 fasting patterns can help establish a long-term lifestyle of both physical health and spiritual renewal, making them powerful tools for transformation in body, mind, and spirit.

From a physical perspective, intermittent fasting promotes the body's natural detoxification processes and cellular repair mechanisms, which can aid in weight management, boost energy levels, and enhance overall health and well-being.

© 2026 Dr. Thomas L. Driver, Ph.D., DMIN. All Rights Reserved.
Published by TLDM Evangelistic Media Network

Many individuals discover that fasting not only helps to decrease cravings and strengthen self-discipline but also enhances mental clarity and emotional stability, leading to overall better well-being.

Intermittent fasting provides regular time for reflection, reading Scripture, worship, and prayer, which can strengthen spiritual awareness and deepen your connection with faith.

Over time, practicing intermittent fasting can lead to a profound and enduring lifestyle transformation, helping individuals regain not only physical strength and health but also spiritual clarity and focus.

For many individuals, this moment serves as a profound and meaningful testament to God's incredible power of renewal and divine presence in their lives.

It helps reinforce their faith, deepen their spiritual devotion, and renew their commitment to their ongoing spiritual journey, inspiring them to continue growing in their relationship with the divine.

Purpose and Benefits

- Physical cleansing and health restoration
- Mental clarity and emotional balance
- Reduced cravings and increased discipline
- Daily spiritual focus
- Long-term lifestyle transformation

My Reflection

Intermittent fasting was essential to my losing more than 50 pounds. Following set fasting times and eating healthy helped me change my eating habits and stop patterns of snacking or emotional eating.

As my body adapted to intermittent fasting, I noticed a significant decrease in cravings and an increase in self-control, which made it easier to make healthier food choices and maintain a consistent routine.

The physical transformation was remarkable: the weight loss led to renewed energy, improved stamina, and a sense of lightness and vitality that I hadn't experienced in years.

As the pounds dropped, my confidence grew, and I found it easier to engage in physical activities and daily tasks. With the reduction in excess weight, I also experienced clearer thinking, better concentration, and a general improvement in my overall well-being.

Along with physical benefits, fasting improved my mental focus and emotional resilience, helping me pursue my goals and strengthen my spiritual awareness for holistic renewal.

This daily fasting routine served as a powerful testament to God's ability to restore and renew, highlighting His divine power at work in everyday acts of devotion.

© 2026 Dr. Thomas L. Driver, Ph.D., DMIN. All Rights Reserved.
Published by TLDM Evangelistic Media Network

7. Specialized Fasts (Bread-Only, Egg-Only, Vegetable-Only, etc.)

During my spiritual and wellness journey, I explored a variety of specialized fasting methods to deepen my faith and support my physical transformation.

For example, I committed to 10 days of eating only eggs, which offered a simple, concentrated source of protein and helped me cut back on processed foods.

I also tried diets focused on bread and vegetables, inspired by biblical examples. These methods helped me stay energized for everyday tasks while supporting detoxification and mental clarity.

Eating whole foods and reducing toxins supported my body's natural cleansing process. Fasting strengthened my discipline, focus, and spiritual growth, helping me renew my faith and enhance my daily routines.

These specialized fasts are patterned after biblical examples of restricted diets and serve as powerful instruments for deepening your spiritual walk when undertaken intentionally and with guidance.

Modified fasting methods have distinct goals and benefits. An egg-only fast, for example, provides protein and is simple, potentially lowering intake of processed foods.

Bread-and-vegetable fasts, based on scriptural traditions, help detoxify the body and provide sufficient energy. Eating only whole, unprocessed foods reduces toxins and supports natural cleansing.

Spiritually, these fasts were not just acts of physical discipline but opportunities for focused consecration and deep internal reflection.

By intentionally limiting your diet, you heightened your awareness of God's provision and redirected your attention from physical cravings to spiritual nourishment.

Fasting can enhance mental and spiritual clarity, increasing creativity and alertness for challenging tasks. These practices help renew spirituality and align daily routines with faith and growth.

These fasts draw upon biblical examples of restricted diets and practices, serving as powerful spiritual tools when guided by the Spirit to deepen one's faith and foster spiritual growth.

Purpose and Benefits

- Targeted physical detox
- Focused spiritual consecration
- Sustained discipline
- Deep internal reflection

My Reflection

These fasts greatly fueled and energized my creativity during various important writing and ministry assignments. They helped me maintain focus, clarity, and mental sharpness as I meticulously prepared devotionals, mentored others, or worked on sermons.

8. Corporate Fasts (Church, Family, Community)

Corporate fasting carries multiplied power, amplifying its spiritual impact. When a group fasts together, not only does unity strengthen, but it also fosters deeper faith and a more profound spiritual atmosphere, creating a collective sense of purpose and reverence.

Examples in Scripture:
- **Nineveh** fasted, and God spared the city (*Jonah 3*).
- **Israel** fasted under Esther's leadership and obtained deliverance (*Esther 4*).
- **The early Church** fasted and received direction from the Holy Spirit (*Acts 13*).

Purpose and Benefits

- Breakthrough for families or ministries
- Unity and spiritual alignment
- Corporate repentance
- Strategic guidance

- Revival and awakening

Corporate fasts unite believers in seeking God's guidance and intervention through shared spiritual discipline. Group fasting shifts focus from individual concerns to collective needs, aiming for breakthrough for families, ministries, or the community.

Corporate fasting serves as a spiritual practice that promotes unity among believers, encourages sincere repentance for personal and collective shortcomings, fosters humility before divine authority, and reinforces reliance on God's guidance and mercy.

Throughout history, such fasts have played a pivotal role in significant events—such as the salvation of Nineveh following Jonah's prophecy, Israel's deliverance from enemies, and divine guidance for the early Christian church, shaping religious communities and inspiring faithfulness.

By fasting together, God's people invite His presence and power to work in profound ways that can ignite revival, inspire strategic insight, and foster a deeper sense of unity among believers.

9. Purpose-Driven Fasts (Specific Topics)

Believers often fast for targeted reasons:
- healing
- deliverance
- clarity

© 2026 Dr. Thomas L. Driver, Ph.D., DMIN. All Rights Reserved.
Published by TLDM Evangelistic Media Network

- financial breakthrough
- marriage restoration
- overcoming addiction
- decision-making
- ministry direction
- spiritual warfare

These fasts are particularly powerful because they effectively combine deliberate intention with sincere intercession, thereby amplifying their overall spiritual significance and making them an especially meaningful practice for those seeking spiritual growth.

Choosing the Right Fast for Your Season

God does not judge your spiritual worth solely on how long you fast; instead, He considers the sincerity of your heart and your intentions. The most meaningful fast is the one that aligns with God's guidance for you in your current season of life, providing spiritual growth and reflection.

Ask yourself:
- What is God drawing me toward?
- What distractions need to be removed?
- What breakthrough am I seeking?
- What level of commitment is sustainable?
- What kind of fast aligns with my physical condition and spiritual needs?

© 2026 Dr. Thomas L. Driver, Ph.D., DMIN. All Rights Reserved.
Published by TLDM Evangelistic Media Network

Fasting is a deeply personal practice that is often guided by one's Spirit, reflecting individual spiritual journeys and inner convictions.

It can serve as a meaningful way to connect with one's inner self, foster spiritual growth, and gain clarity or insight during times of reflection and self-discipline.

Conclusion: Your Fast is Your Offering

Every fast, regardless of its type or duration, is ultimately a deeply personal act rooted in faith. The core value lies not just in the act itself but in the sincerity and genuine intention behind one's abstention, reflecting a spiritual commitment.

Each individual's fast reflects their personal faith, being appreciated for its sincerity and dedication rather than how long it lasts or the specific method used.

Fasting provides an opportunity for individuals to reflect, grow spiritually, and commit to God, helping each person deepen their relationship with God in a way that suits their unique situation and beliefs.

Fasting isn't meant to impress heaven; rather, it is a sincere invitation for heaven's presence to enter your life, creating room for spiritual growth and a closer relationship with God.

© 2026 Dr. Thomas L. Driver, Ph.D., DMIN. All Rights Reserved.
Published by TLDM Evangelistic Media Network

Whatever fast you choose, do it with:
- sincerity
- discipline
- Scripture
- prayer
- humility
- expectation

When you present your faith as worship, God responds with power. Approaching fasting with a sincere heart of reverence and adoration invites God's presence to move uniquely in your life.

View fasting not only as a religious practice but as a sacred act to honor God with your body, desires, and time. This approach encourages spiritual growth, guidance, and a deeper connection with God.

As your fast turns into an act of devotion, God responds by meeting you in your surrender, often revealing new insights, providing clarity, and releasing strength that you couldn't summon on your own.

Worshipful fasting invites spiritual change by seeking God's power in your life. Dedicating your fast as an act of reverence aligns you with God's will, offering guidance, clarity, and renewed faith.

Chapter 6:
Preparing for a Fast:
Setting Your Spirit, Mind, and Body in Alignment with God

A powerful fast doesn't begin when you stop eating. It starts when you intentionally seek God. Preparation is often the key difference between a spiritually transformative fast and one that feels aimless or overwhelming.

Similar to how an athlete trains hard for a race and a soldier prepares for battle, a believer must intentionally ready their body, mind, and spirit to embrace a time of consecration, fostering spiritual growth and renewed dedication.

In this chapter, we explore how to prepare holistically—spiritually, mentally, physically, emotionally, and practically—so your fast is sustainable, meaningful, and guided by the Holy Spirit.

1. Preparing Your Heart: The Spiritual Foundation

Fasting is mainly a deeply spiritual act that involves aligning the heart before the body can follow. It starts with heartfelt prayer, genuine surrender, and an expectation of spiritual growth and connection.

A. Seek God's Purpose for the Fast

Ask the Lord:
- "What are you calling me to lay down?"
- "What breakthrough do you want to bring?"
- "How do you want to transform me during this fast?"

When God reveals the purpose, the fast gains clear direction and increased authority, enabling them to move forward with confidence and purpose.

B. Enter With Humility

Scripture reminds us:
"I humbled myself with fasting."
—Psalm 35:13, NKJV

Humility creates space for God to communicate and work within our lives. Approach the fast not with arrogance or strictness, but with a humble, teachable, and surrendered heart that seeks His guidance.

C. Repent and Release

Fasting tends to be most effective when the heart is pure and unburdened. Before starting a fast, it's important to prepare both the body and mind to ensure the process is beneficial and harmonious.

- forgive offenses
- release bitterness
- confess sin
- ask for cleansing
- surrender distractions

Repentance can be likened to preparing the soil of our hearts, a thorough process that involves cleansing ourselves from impurities, cultivating humility, and engaging in deep reflection.

By undertaking this process, we make our hearts more receptive and open, creating the fertile ground necessary for God's new blessings to take root, grow, and flourish within us, ultimately transforming our lives and drawing us closer to Him.

When we truly repent from the heart, we open ourselves fully to divine grace. This grace then has the opportunity to take root deeply within us, growing stronger over time and flourishing in every aspect of our lives, guiding us toward transformation and renewal.

D. Build Expectation

Faith serves as the driving force behind fasting. When you dedicate yourself to this spiritual discipline, you can confidently expect that God will offer you the necessary strength to persevere, guide you with divine wisdom along your journey, and bestow blessings upon you as you seek to grow closer to Him through this practice.

- reveal
- refine
- restore
- break chains
- strengthen
- renew
- speak

Expectation differs from arrogance; it represents a confident trust that, when sincerely sought in private moments, God will reveal guidance and strength to those who seek Him earnestly.

This statement is a personal assurance grounded in faith, representing a deep reliance on God's unwavering promises to support, guide, and direct every aspect of your life, providing comfort and confidence in His divine plan.

2. Preparing Your Mind: Renewing Your Thoughts

During a fast, the mind often becomes the main area of struggle, emphasizing the need for comprehensive mental preparation. Strengthening your mental resilience helps you resist temptations, stay focused, and have a more effective and enduring fasting experience.

Techniques like mindfulness, positive visualization, and keeping your goals in mind can all help you overcome the mental hurdles of fasting.

A. Decide Before You Begin

The most successful fasts are predetermined. Set:
- the type of fast
- the start and end dates
- your prayer schedule
- your Scripture reading plan
- your worship rhythms

When decisions are made in advance, the mind experiences a profound sense of calmness and stability. This proactive planning fosters a clear understanding of the situation, allowing individuals to evaluate all relevant factors thoroughly.

Such preparation leads to a firm commitment to the chosen course of action, which can help mitigate doubts and reduce emotional turbulence.

Additionally, this approach minimizes uncertainty, enabling a person to maintain focus and confidence over time, even in complex or unpredictable circumstances.

This proactive approach not only helps individuals maintain focus and confidence but also equips them with the necessary skills and mindset to effectively navigate a variety of challenges. By fostering a steady and composed demeanor, individuals are better prepared to handle obstacles with resilience and clarity.

B. Anticipate Challenges

Prepare mentally for:
- hunger pangs
- fatigue
- irritability
- emotional sensitivity
- spiritual resistance
- cravings

These are normal; they do not indicate failure but rather show that your flesh is adapting to the authority of your spirit.

C. Replace Negative Thoughts

During fasting, the enemy often whispers:
- "This is too hard."
- "It isn't working."

© 2026 Dr. Thomas L. Driver, Ph.D., DMIN. All Rights Reserved.
Published by TLDM Evangelistic Media Network

- "You should quit."
- "This sacrifice doesn't matter."

Combat those lies with truth:
"My grace is sufficient for you."
—2 Corinthians 12:9, NKJV

"I can do all things through Christ who strengthens me."
—Philippians 4:13, NKJV

Mental discipline strengthens spiritual momentum.

3. Preparing Your Body: The Physical Component

Fasting affects the entire system of the body. Proper preparation is essential to facilitate a smoother and safer transition, particularly during longer or modified fasting periods.

A. Taper Before You Fast

A few days before your fast:
- reduce caffeine
- reduce sugar
- eat lighter meals
- hydrate consistently
- avoid heavy, greasy foods
- increase fruits and vegetables

B. Hydrate Thoroughly

Water is crucial for staying properly hydrated, especially during fasting. It's advisable to start increasing your fluid intake days before fasting to ensure complete hydration and optimal body function.

Adequate hydration plays a crucial role in supporting essential bodily functions, such as circulation, temperature regulation, and nutrient transport.

It also helps alleviate symptoms of dehydration like fatigue, dizziness, and headaches, while preparing and priming your system for fasting by ensuring that your organs and metabolic processes are functioning optimally.

If your fasting regimen permits liquids, drinking enough water can help prevent dehydration, support bodily functions, and make your fasting experience more manageable.

- herbal teas
- light broths
- water with lemon
- electrolyte water
- diluted juices (if appropriate)

Proper hydration promotes optimal brain function and physical performance by ensuring that cells function efficiently.

Staying properly hydrated can sharpen your thinking and boost your alertness. It also helps fend off tiredness and other dehydration-related problems, so you can recover more quickly and maintain your energy for longer.

C. Prepare Your Environment

Remove temptations:

- snacks
- sweets
- trigger foods
- unnecessary distractions

Create a fasting-friendly atmosphere:

- worship music available
- Bible nearby
- journal ready
- quiet place for prayer
- a comfortable prayer chair or prayer room

Your environment supports your discipline.

D. Rest

During fasting, your body uses energy in various ways. Ensure you get enough sleep both before and during the fast. Feeling tired is normal and part of the process, not a sign of failure.

© 2026 Dr. Thomas L. Driver, Ph.D., DMIN. All Rights Reserved.
Published by TLDM Evangelistic Media Network

4. Preparing Your Schedule: Planning for Success

Fasting requires meticulous planning and preparation. Without a thoughtful and organized approach, the days may slip by without offering meaningful opportunities for deep spiritual growth, reflection, and internal development.

A. Block Out Time for Prayer

Set specific times for:

- morning prayer
- lunchtime prayer (even if you're not eating)
- evening reflection
- Scripture meditation
- worship moments
- journaling

Prayer plays a crucial role in fasting, forming the basis for actual personal change and spiritual growth. While fasting involves physical abstention, prayer strengthens your connection to faith and the reason for your fast.

Consistent prayer can offer guidance, strength, clarity, and help you reflect and seek wisdom on your journey. Setting aside time for prayer in the morning, midday, and evening encourages reflection, gratitude, and spiritual connection.

This ongoing communication with God transforms fasting from merely a physical act into a deeply meaningful spiritual experience, enriching one's faith and fostering a closer relationship with the divine.

B. Limit Distractions

During fasting, consider reducing:

- social media
- unnecessary conversations
- television
- entertainment
- idle activities

Replace distractions with Scripture, prayer, rest, and worship to deepen your spiritual connection and foster inner peace. Consider dedicating specific times for these practices daily to cultivate a more profound sense of calm and spiritual growth.

C. Inform Those Who Need to Know

You are not obligated to publicly announce your fast; however, it is advisable to inform others about it to promote transparency and understanding within the community.

- your spouse
- your ministry team
- your accountability partner

…helps them support your journey and reduces unnecessary pressure.

5. Preparing Your Spirit Through Scripture
Fasting without Scripture is incomplete.

Choose passages to meditate on:
- Psalm 51 (repentance)
- Isaiah 58 (true fasting)
- Daniel 10 (Revelation)
- Matthew 4 (Jesus' fast)
- Acts 13 (Holy Spirit direction)
- Joel 2 (returning to God)

Reading through a single Gospel during a fast can be a profoundly impactful experience, particularly with the texts of Mark or John. These Gospels offer rich narratives and insights that deepen one's spiritual reflection and understanding.

6. Preparing with Purpose: Identify What You are Fasting For

Purpose gives clear direction to your prayers. You may be fasting for various reasons, such as seeking guidance, expressing reverence, demonstrating devotion, or asking for specific needs.

- spiritual breakthrough
- clarity and direction
- healing
- deliverance

- family restoration
- ministry preparation
- a renewed prayer life
- fresh vision
- emotional healing
- physical healing
- financial breakthrough
- increased sensitivity to the Holy Spirit

Write your purpose in a journal before your fast begins.

7. My Personal Approach: Lifestyle of Preparation

Over the years, I've come to realize that preparation is just as vital as the race itself. My routine includes a series of dedicated steps that I personalize to ensure I am ready for every challenge.

A. Spiritual Readiness

Before I start any fast, I dedicate time to seeking the Lord's guidance and clarity. Whether I am observing a brief 24-hour Sabbath fast or committing to a more extended 10-day Daniel-type fast, I make it a point to consciously seek His direction and wisdom beforehand.

B. Mental Focus

Throughout my time in the military, I learned that success depends on thorough preparation. I applied that same discipline to my fasting approach—carefully planning my strategy, eliminating distractions, and deliberately sharpening my focus so I could fully achieve my spiritual goals.

C. Physical Wisdom

By practicing different fasting methods such as egg-only, vegetable, bread, liquid fasts, and 18:6 intermittent fasting, I gradually trained my body to improve both safety and effectiveness.

D. Emotional Stability

Before starting a fast, I intentionally take time to reduce stress, release anger, let go of frustration, and overcome disappointment, calming my mind and emotions.

This intentional process helps me achieve a precise, focused mental state, creating an open, receptive environment for connecting with spiritual guidance and presence.

Preparation is not optional—it is a spiritual strategy.

Conclusion: Preparation Positions You for Victory

A well-prepared fast leads to:

- deeper prayer
- clearer revelation
- stronger discipline
- fewer physical challenges
- greater focus
- sustained results
- a heart fully yielded to God

When you thoughtfully prepare your heart, mind, body, and spirit, you approach the fast from a place of strength and serenity rather than struggle and resistance.

Fasting becomes a heartfelt act of devotion—an inspiring offer from the soul—that opens the door to profound change and renewal.

Fasting is more than simply skipping the initial meal of the day; it encompasses that deeply meaningful moment when you genuinely direct your heart and mind to the divine, sincerely saying, *"Lord, I am yours,"* acknowledging your devotion and surrender.

Chapter 7:
The Spiritual Power of Fasting: Understanding What Happens in the Unseen Realm

Fasting serves both as a physical practice and a spiritual discipline. At the same time, experiencing hunger and stress, a profound inner process unfolds, fostering self-awareness and spiritual growth.

Scripture shows that when believers fast with sincerity, humility, and prayer, unseen movements occur—movements that change circumstances, break chains, reveal truths, and bring about victory.

This chapter explores the spiritual aspect of fasting—what occurs in the unseen realm, why fasting enhances spiritual authority, and how God reacts when His people choose consecration over comfort.

1. Fasting Weakens the Flesh and Strengthens the Spirit

Your physical hunger isn't the true battleground in this spiritual struggle. Instead, the real fight takes place within—your flesh, which includes the parts of you that resist God, seek comfort above all, and crave control over your life. These inner urges and desires are the true battleground where your faith is tested and strengthened.

Jesus taught:
"The spirit indeed is willing, but the flesh is weak."
—Matthew 26:41, NKJV

Fasting tests the flesh's restraint, helping deepen one's personal relationship with God by quieting inner urges that sometimes conflict with spiritual commitments.

- cravings
- impulses
- attachments
- habits
- distractions

When the flesh weakens, the spirit awakens. Prayer becomes more focused, Scripture becomes more alive, and you begin to sense God's presence more clearly.

© 2026 Dr. Thomas L. Driver, Ph.D., DMIN. All Rights Reserved.
Published by TLDM Evangelistic Media Network

My Reflection

Repeated experience with various fasting practices—such as intermittent fasting (18:6), weekly Sabbath fasting, and occasional extended specialized fasts—has consistently demonstrated this undeniable truth.

When the flesh grows quiet, the Spirit speaks loudly.

For me personally, fasting has become an essential and transformative practice during seasons of change. It has profoundly helped me to hear God's guidance more clearly and distinctly as I navigate through new chapters and challenges in life, providing spiritual clarity and strength.

Fasting has increased my awareness of spiritual struggles, allowing me to identify challenges early. This greater sensitivity and trust in God empower me to lead ministries with confidence, inspire me to write uplifting books, guide students through mentoring, and confront crises with faith and bravery.

2. Fasting Increases Sensitivity to the Holy Spirit

Fasting does not force God to speak—fasting helps you hear. This means that fasting isn't about trying to make God say something or manipulate Him into action. Instead, it's about making yourself more receptive and attentive to what God is already communicating.

By setting aside distractions and physical comforts, your mind and spirit become more precise and more focused, making it easier to notice God's gentle guidance and presence.

From my own experience, fasting isn't about making God speak more, but rather about helping me tune out my desires and daily distractions.

For instance, when I fast, Scripture feels brighter, and I notice God's guidance in new ways. It's like fasting brings my heart closer to God's, making it easier to listen carefully and understand His will more clearly.

The Holy Spirit guides us, but daily distractions like social media and stress can interfere with our ability to hear and understand divine guidance.

Examples from Scripture:
- Paul and Barnabas received their missionary assignment while fasting (*Acts 13:2*).
- Daniel received angelic revelation after fasting (*Daniel 10:12–14*).
- Anna recognized the Messiah through a lifetime of fasting (*Luke 2:36–38*).

What Happens During Fasting
- Your discernment sharpens
- Your thoughts become clearer

- Your spiritual instincts become more accurate
- Your decisions align with God's will
- Your emotional reactions soften

3. Fasting Produces Breakthrough in Spiritual Warfare

Some breakthroughs do not happen through prayer alone. Jesus Himself said:

"This kind does not go out except by prayer and fasting." —Matthew 17:21, NKJV

Some battles require increased spiritual authority.

- Prayer connects you to God.
- Fasting disconnects you from the flesh.
- Together, they dismantle demonic resistance.

Atmospheric Shift

During a fast, the spiritual atmosphere surrounding you undergoes a profound transformation, leading to an increased sense of connection, mindfulness, and inner clarity.

This process allows you to become more deeply attuned to your inner self and the world around you, fostering greater awareness of your thoughts, emotions, and the subtle energies at play within and around you.

- oppression lifts

- confusion breaks
- demonic interference weakens
- generational patterns lose influence
- inner torment subsides

My Reflection

During periods of intense spiritual challenges—whether they involve legal issues, ministry obstacles, emotional struggles, or financial difficulties—fasting provided me with clarity, a sense of peace, and personal breakthroughs that helped me navigate through those tough times.

Fasting fortified my resolve, enabling me to stand firm against the enemy's attempts to overpower me. It disrupted old cycles of weakness, silenced doubt and fear, and restored my sense of purpose and clear direction.

Reflecting on that period, the journey was tough. Legal issues caused anxiety, ministry demands were overwhelming, emotional struggles sapped hope, and financial problems threatened stability.

Amid the chaos, fasting provided a vital refuge. With each day of sacrifice, I observed minor changes—calm replacing anxiety and hope returning where despair had been.

Rather than reacting impulsively, I chose to respond with wisdom and patience. Oppressive thoughts eased, and the confusion that once clouded my choices cleared, revealing a clear path ahead.

The cycles of defeat and discouragement no longer held sway. Through fasting, I uncovered an inner resilience strength rooted in faith—that helped me persevere even when surrender seemed easier.

The most significant change, however, was spiritual. My prayers grew stronger and more focused, and I felt a renewed connection to God.

The distractions of everyday life faded into the background, allowing me to hear God's voice more clearly. Fasting showed me that spiritual discipline leads to real breakthroughs, strengthening my faith and resilience.

Fasting is spiritual warfare done God's way.

4. Fasting Turns Prayer into Power

Prayer is mighty on its own, and when paired with fasting, it becomes an even more uplifting and divine experience, filling us with spiritual strength and purpose.

In Scripture:

- Daniel's prayers released angelic movement
- Jesus overcame Satan through Scripture and fasting
- Jehoshaphat's fast led Israel into miraculous deliverance
- Nineveh's fast turned judgment into mercy

When fasting is added to prayer:
- faith intensifies
- conviction deepens
- boldness increases
- distractions diminish
- the Word of God penetrates more deeply

Prayer is naturally a heartfelt way to connect spiritually and seek guidance. When paired with fasting—where we abstain from food or other pleasures—it can make that connection even stronger.

This wonderful combination helps deepen your bond with the divine, boosts your focus and devotion, and often brings about meaningful personal growth and inspiring spiritual insights.

5. Fasting Breaks Chains and Releases Deliverance

Isaiah 58:6 reveals God's heart:
> *"Is this not the fast that I have chosen:*
> *To loose the bonds of wickedness,*
> *To undo the heavy burdens,*
> *To let the oppressed go free,*
> *And that you break every yoke?"*
> —Isaiah 58:6, NKJV

Fasting:
- breaks addictions
- uproots bondage
- dismantles oppression
- releases spiritual freedom
- heals the brokenhearted
- restores emotional balance

Many believers wage their battles through physical or emotional means, unaware that the actual root is spiritual. Fasting serves to expose and eradicate these spiritual roots.

My Reflection

I have seen firsthand how fasting brings deliverance—breaking habits, lifting emotional burdens, and removing anxiety. Fasting exposes what weighs you down and helps you overcome it.

In my spiritual journey, fasting has freed me from patterns and anxieties that seemed insurmountable, giving me clarity and peace.

For me, fasting is not just a religious practice but a profound means of drawing closer to God, deepening my spiritual connection, confronting and overcoming spiritual struggles, and experiencing genuine healing and freedom.

It aligns with the powerful promise of Isaiah 58:6, emphasizing that true fasting involves more than outward rituals—it encompasses a sincere journey toward inner transformation, renewal, and divine intimacy.

6. Fasting Produces Revelation and Divine Insight

Daniel is the clearest example. After 21 days of fasting:

"Then he said to me, 'Do not fear, Daniel... from the moment you set your heart... your words were heard.'"
—Daniel 10:12, NKJV

Daniel's fast unlocked:

- prophetic revelation
- angelic visitation
- divine interpretation
- understanding of spiritual conflict

Revelation is the outcome of a surrendered spirit. When your mind is clarified and open to divine guidance, God can speak into your destiny, revealing your deeper purpose and direction.

Personal Testimony

Many of my most creative and effective ideas for books, sermon outlines, ministry plans, business strategies, and academic breakthroughs often come during fasting, as it helps clear my mind and fosters new insights.

I am deeply thankful that God has influenced my thinking, clarified my purpose, and revealed new solutions. He has guided me through difficulties and brightened my path with wisdom and grace.

7. Fasting Strengthens Spiritual Authority

Authority is not loudness—it is alignment with God.

Jesus demonstrated this after fasting:
"He taught them as one having authority."
—Matthew 7:29, NKJV

Authority increases when:

- the spirit is strong
- the flesh is subdued
- prayer is fervent
- Scripture is alive
- the believer walks in holiness

Fasting enhances and personally empowers the believer's authority over various spiritual and worldly influences, strengthening their ability to overcome challenges and deepen their faith.

- temptation
- fear
- confusion
- demonic schemes

- emotional immaturity
- doubt

Spiritual authority grows in proportion to spiritual commitment. The more a believer dedicates themselves to God through prayer, scripture study, holy living, and fasting, the greater their spiritual authority becomes.

Spiritual consecration means intentionally distancing oneself from distractions, temptations, and anything that could block one's relationship with God.

The more someone pursues holiness and aligns their life with God's will, the better they become at overcoming challenges such as fear, confusion, demonic schemes, emotional immaturity, and doubt.

Fasting is said to help believers overcome challenges. As individuals dedicate themselves through fasting and other spiritual practices, they become more receptive to God's guidance, gain clarity in their calling, and find peace during transitions.

Essentially, the level of spiritual authority a believer has is directly related to how much they have dedicated themselves to God and surrendered their own desires to His will.

8. Fasting Repositions the Believer in God's Perfect Will

Fasting isn't about gaining God's favor, but about aligning your life with His will. By fasting, you intentionally surrender your personal plans, opinions, desires, and distractions, creating space for spiritual focus and growth.

What follows:
- clarity in calling
- direction for decisions
- confirmation of assignments
- peace in transition
- sensitivity to God's timing

Fasting brings spiritual alignment.

My Reflection

During significant transitions—such as facing personal challenges, improving health, experiencing business growth, or working on the writing and publication of several books—fasting offered a sense of stability and helped me stay aligned with my broader goals.

It served as a safeguard against impulsive, emotionally driven decisions and allowed me to gain clearer insight into God's plan for my life.

9. Fasting Builds Discipline and Strengthens Character

Fasting strengthens virtues such as:
- patience
- endurance

- self-control
- humility
- gratitude
- intentionality

These qualities—patience, endurance, self-control, humility, gratitude, and intentionality—help shape spiritual maturity by guiding actions, responses to challenges, and reliance on God.

Fasting helps develop self-control, humility before God, gratitude for daily needs, and a disciplined mindset by intentionally giving up physical comforts.

Over time, this practice not only strengthens character but also aligns the heart and mind more closely with God's plans, leading to greater spiritual growth and resilience in the face of life's trials.

Conclusion:
Unseen Realm Responds When You Fast

Fasting is more than just a human act; it embodies a profound supernatural exchange that transcends the physical realm, connecting the spiritual and cosmic energies in a sacred act of surrender and communication.

The moment you begin fasting, a transformative shift takes place in the heavens, signaling a divine response and acknowledgment of your spiritual commitment.

A break occurs within the spirit, leading to a profound awakening within the soul and a strengthening of the mind. This process also helps realign your life with your true calling, bringing greater purpose and clarity.

† Fasting may weaken the body, **but it empowers the spirit.**

† It magnifies the voice of God.

† It quiets the noise of life.

† It unleashes spiritual authority.

† It dismantles strongholds.

† It prepares the believer for purpose.

† When believers fast, heaven moves.

Chapter 8:
Fasting and Prayer:
Divine Partnership that Unlocks Breakthrough

Fasting is a powerful practice that can significantly enhance spiritual growth. Prayers are equally potent, serving as a vital means of communicating with the divine.

When these two spiritual disciplines are combined, they forge one of the most powerful and transformative partnerships in a believer's life, amplifying their faith, resilience, and connection to a higher power.

Fasting without prayer becomes just a diet and lacks spiritual meaning. Conversely, prayer alone often lacks the depth and the transformative power that fasting offers. When combined, fasting and prayer form a deep spiritual discipline that fosters inner growth and connection.

But when fasting and prayer come together, they create spiritual clarity, divine power, and supernatural breakthrough.

This chapter reveals why prayer and fasting must be inseparable, how they work together, and how this divine partnership transforms believers from the inside out.

1. Why Fasting Must Always Be Paired with Prayer

In Scripture, fasting is rarely mentioned without prayer. Throughout the Bible, whenever people or groups fasted, it was almost always combined with sincere prayer.

One notable example is Anna, the prophetess, who *"never left the temple but worshiped night and day, fasting and praying"* (Luke 2:37). Her devotion shows how fasting and prayer are closely linked disciplines for seeking God and strengthening spiritual connection.

These spiritual disciplines are closely linked: Daniel fasted and prayed for insight (Daniel 9–10), Ezra sought guidance and protection through both practices (Ezra 8:23), and Nehemiah interceded for his people using fasting and prayer (Nehemiah 1:4).

Similarly, the early church in Antioch gathered together regularly to fast and pray as they sought divine guidance before making significant decisions, as documented in Acts 13:2–3.

In the Bible, fasting is more than just abstaining from food; it is often accompanied by prayer and meditation to seek God's guidance, deepen one's spiritual connection, and invite His presence into one's life.

Fasting and prayer together enhance spiritual clarity, power, and transformation; fasting alone is less impactful, and prayer becomes deeper through fasting.

It is always a partnership:

- Daniel fasted and prayed (*Daniel 9–10. NKJV*)
- Ezra fasted and prayed (*Ezra 8:23, NKJV*)
- Nehemiah fasted and prayed (*Nehemiah 1:4, NKJV*)
- Anna fasted and prayed (*Luke 2:37, NKJV*)
- The church in Antioch fasted and prayed (*Acts 13:2–3, NKJV*)

† Fasting opens the spirit.

† Prayer fills the spirit.

† Fasting empties the soul.

† Prayer nourishes the soul.

† Fasting removes distractions.

† Prayer connects you to God.

Fasting without prayer is incomplete because, throughout the Bible and in spiritual practice, fasting and prayer are meant to go hand in hand, supporting and enhancing one another in a sacred partnership to deepen faith and spiritual growth.

Fasting cleanses the heart for spiritual growth, while prayer strengthens discipline and deepens connection with the divine. Together, they offer a balanced way to nurture one's spiritual journey.

In today's busy world, finding time to step away from distractions can be more challenging than ever. Just giving up food or comforts without truly engaging in focused prayer might miss the real purpose—deepening our connection with God.

Fasting, combined with intentional prayer, fosters deeper spiritual growth, clarity, and a stronger relationship with God, helping you face the challenges of modern life with more peace and purpose.

2. Fasting Intensifies Prayer

When you enter a period of fasting, your prayers tend to become more vivid, sincere, and deeply guided by the Spirit.

This meaningful transformation occurs because fasting helps diminish the influence of the flesh—the part of us that can sometimes hold us back or distract us—and elevates the spirit, fostering a stronger, more intimate connection with God.

During fasting, the mind and body become more aligned with spiritual pursuits, allowing your communication with divine principles to grow richer and more profound.

During fasting:

- your emotions soften
- your motives purify
- your mind quiets
- your heart opens
- your spirit becomes sensitive

This heightened sensitivity enhances the depth and significance of prayer. It inspires us to approach prayer with sincere surrender and humility, rather than relying solely on our own willpower or personal strength.

Prayer During Fasting Often Includes:

- repentance
- worship
- surrender
- listening
- intercession
- thanksgiving
- spiritual warfare

Fasting elevates all these forms of prayer.

© 2026 Dr. Thomas L. Driver, Ph.D., DMIN. All Rights Reserved.
Published by TLDM Evangelistic Media Network

3. Fasting Makes Space for God to Speak

Many believers want to hear God more clearly, but their lives are too crowded. The noise of daily routine, technology, emotions, stress, and responsibilities often muffles the Spirit's voice.

Fasting helps clear away distractions, creating a peaceful silence that invites prayer to be filled with God's divine guidance, insight, and wisdom.

In the quiet wilderness, Jesus was not overwhelmed by crowds or distractions. He chose to fast, and during this time, the loving voice of the Father guided, strengthened, and prepared Him for His essential mission.

Similarly, during fasting:

- Scripture speaks more clearly
- the Holy Spirit's whispers become louder
- God reveals hidden things
- direction becomes sharper
- insights become deeper

Prayer turns fasting into revelation.

4. Fasting Strengthens Intercession

Intercession is a form of spiritual warfare that requires perseverance, clarity, compassion, and authority—qualities that are deepened through fasting.

© 2026 Dr. Thomas L. Driver, Ph.D., DMIN. All Rights Reserved.
Published by TLDM Evangelistic Media Network

During fasting, your heart becomes more compassionate toward others. Your empathy deepens. Your prayers shift from being self-focused to kingdom-focused. You start to carry others' burdens with greater spiritual sensitivity.

Intercession During Fasting Breaks:
- generational patterns
- addictions
- spiritual blindness
- emotional bondage
- demonic oppression
- family conflict
- confusion and deception

Fasting substantially broadens the scope and intensity of your intercession, significantly boosting your authority and effectiveness in prayer.

5. Fasting Positions You for Breakthrough

While certain breakthroughs can be achieved through prayer alone, there are situations where prayer must be coupled with fasting to bring about lasting change.

Certain issues—such as generational patterns, addictions, emotional difficulties, and spiritual challenges—can persist despite consistent prayer.

In these cases, the added discipline of fasting amplifies your intercession and increases your spiritual authority, creating a powerful atmosphere for breakthrough.

Combining fasting with prayer can help overcome ongoing difficulties by providing insight, healing, direction, and emotional refreshment. According to Jesus, certain obstacles can only be resolved through both prayer and fasting.

Jesus made this distinction clear:
"This kind does not go out except by prayer and fasting."
—Matthew 17:21, NKJV

Some strongholds—such as deeply rooted behaviors or persistent spiritual resistance—cannot be easily broken by prayer alone, as they often require sustained effort, specific strategies, and sometimes additional forms of support to be effectively overcome.

To effectively tackle them, it's often necessary to combine prayer with fasting, which enhances spiritual focus and discipline, resulting in a more potent way to confront and break down these barriers.

Breakthrough Areas that Often Respond to Fasting + Prayer

- spiritual clarity
- healing
- guidance

- emotional restoration
- deliverance
- family transformation
- forgiveness
- breaking soul ties
- hearing God's voice
- victory over temptation
- overcoming spiritual attacks

Prayer strengthens faith through personal connection with the divine, while fasting enhances spiritual discipline. Together, they foster perseverance and insight.

6. Fasting Deepens Worship

Worship during fasting takes on a deeper, more personal significance. As physical desires diminish and distractions decrease, the spirit becomes more alert and receptive, allowing for greater focus and connection during prayer and reflection.

This increased awareness deepens the feeling of God's presence, allowing a more personal and meaningful relationship with Him. As a result, it strengthens your spiritual connection and renews your sense of devotion.

Worship becomes:
- heartfelt
- reflective

- sincere
- powerful
- transformative

Since your heart is more sensitive, true worship goes beyond just singing and becomes an act of surrender. During fasting and prayer, your physical desires and distractions often lessen, allowing your spirit to become more receptive and aware.

This heightened sensitivity means that worship goes beyond just singing songs or reciting prayers. Instead, it transforms into a deeper experience where you intentionally offer your thoughts, emotions, and will to God.

Surrendering during worship means fully opening your heart to God's presence, releasing your own plans, and placing complete trust in Him. It is an act of humility that recognizes your dependence on God and offers not just words but your entire heart, mind, and spirit.

As your spiritual connection strengthens, worship becomes an authentic and heartfelt expression of love. This genuine form of prayer can have a significant impact, nurturing a deeper, more meaningful relationship with God.

My Reflection

My weekly Sabbath fasts always deepened my worship and brought a stronger sense of God's presence, whether I gave up food, observed silence, or concentrated on prayer.

As my physical needs decreased, I became more spiritually aware, making worship more heartfelt. Sabbath fasts transformed songs and Scripture into emotional, vivid experiences.

Fasting heightened my awareness of God's presence, making each Sabbath feel refreshing. Songs moved me, Scriptures resonated deeply, and I realized fasting helped me notice God more.

7. Praying the Word During a Fast

Scripture serves as the Spirit's sword, and fasting enhances the power and impact of God's Word. When we fast, we become more receptive to spiritual truths, allowing God's Word to reach deeper into our hearts and minds.

Fasting not only helps us sharpen our focus and strengthens our reliance on God, but also enhances our ability to discern His guidance more clearly.

Through dedicated prayer and reflective contemplation during fasting, we often experience greater clarity, leading to meaningful personal transformation and spiritual growth.

The Word not only guides us but also transforms our attitudes, brings healing, and gives us strength. Familiar verses can offer fresh meaning and make God's promises feel personal, enriching our worship and connection with Him.

Powerful Scriptures to Pray While Fasting

† Psalm 51—cleansing

† Isaiah 58—true fasting

† Psalm 63—hunger for God

† Daniel 10—revelation

† Romans 12—living sacrifice

† Matthew 4—resisting temptation

† Acts 13—Holy Spirit guidance

Praying Scripture is a wonderful way to deepen your relationship with God. It allows your heart to connect more profoundly with His truth and helps you gently confront and overcome the lies and deceptions that the enemy spreads. This meaningful practice nurtures your faith and draws you nearer to His love.

8. Listening Prayer: Most Overlooked Part of Fasting

Prayer is more than just talking to God; it's also about taking the time to listen to Him and opening our hearts to His guidance and wisdom.

While it's natural to share our requests, concerns, and thanks with God, it's just as valuable to embrace moments of quietness and stillness, especially when fasting.

© 2026 Dr. Thomas L. Driver, Ph.D., DMIN. All Rights Reserved.
Published by TLDM Evangelistic Media Network

These peaceful pauses serve to strengthen and deepen our connection and understanding, allowing us to reflect, regenerate, and foster a more meaningful bond.

Listening prayer entails intentionally pausing, cultivating patience, and surrendering our personal agendas to create space for God's voice to be heard, allowing for a deeper connection and understanding.

During these quiet moments, we have the opportunity to truly understand His divine guidance, willingly accept correction when needed, and find encouragement to continue forward.

This experience is similar to the gentle whisper Elijah heard on Mount Horeb, which brought clarity and reassurance amidst the silence.

By embracing both speaking and listening in prayer, we foster a deeper relationship with God and become more open to His subtle yet powerful guidance.

Listening prayer requires:
- quietness
- stillness
- patience
- surrender

Silence during fasting can offer profound insight, as it is often in these quiet moments that God provides subtle guidance and presence.

Listening prayer helps you receive:

- direction
- correction
- affirmation
- wisdom
- strategy
- comfort
- insight
- creativity

During fasting, I wake at 3 AM to pray, finding the early hours calm and free of distractions. This quiet time helps me connect with God and receive guidance and comfort through prayer.

Engaging in prayer at this time encourages attentiveness to guidance, wisdom, and creativity, not through effort but through presence and openness.

Like Elijah recognizing God's voice in a soft whisper, silent prayer in the early-morning quiet often provides deep insights and a sense of God's presence—benefits that can be missed amid the busyness of everyday life.

Through attentive stillness, I gained insights that were lost in my busy thoughts. In these quiet moments, I clearly sensed God's guidance, correction, and affirmation.

Wisdom and creative solutions came to me not through effort, but through quiet receptivity. Like Elijah hearing God in a gentle whisper, I find that silent prayer opens space for subtle yet powerful guidance.

9. Journaling Prayer: Capturing What God Reveals

Journaling is a powerful tool during fasting because it helps document your thoughts, feelings, physical sensations, and progress throughout the process.

- what God reveals
- what you're praying for
- What breakthroughs occur
- what Scriptures come alive
- what emotions arise
- what the Spirit impresses on your heart

Many years later, your journal remains a powerful testament to God's unwavering loyalty and the consistent guidance provided to you throughout your journey, serving as a reminder of His steadfast presence in your life.

© 2026 Dr. Thomas L. Driver, Ph.D., DMIN. All Rights Reserved.
Published by TLDM Evangelistic Media Network

My Reflection

In times when I faced loss, change, stress, and spiritual challenges, my journal became a space for personal reflection. While fasting and praying, I recorded everything I felt was shown to me.

During difficult times, I faced betrayal and legal battles that made my journey feel even heavier and more complex. Being let down by people I trusted deeply left a mark on me, causing me to question my faith, but it also taught me resilience.

The pain of broken trust frequently left me feeling isolated and alone, yet it also served as a catalyst that drew me closer to God. In these moments of vulnerability, I sought His comfort, guidance, and wisdom, finding strength in His presence and deepening my faith.

By consistently journaling my prayers and Scriptures, I not only documented moments of God's support and intervention but also created a detailed record of my ongoing spiritual growth and development over the years.

These entries documented how I navigated various legal and personal challenges, offering tangible reminders of God's unwavering faithfulness during times of loss, betrayal, and change.

As I revisited these pages, I could see clear evidence of transformation—a shift from feeling isolated and questioning my faith to developing resilience and a deeper trust in God's wisdom and presence.

My reflections marked a journey of healing and renewal, mapping out how my relationship with God matured and my perspective shifted from pain to purpose.

Regular journaling led to a significant lifestyle shift for me. Writing down prayers and meaningful Scriptures helped process emotions, notice progress, and follow spiritual guidance.

This practice gave me clarity, strength, and helped me form new habits for ministry, as shown in my journal documenting God's faithfulness.

Reflecting on those pages, I saw how God's guidance has beautifully shaped my life, filling it with purpose and preparing me wholeheartedly for ministry.

10. Synergy of Fasting and Prayer

Prayer connects me to heaven; fasting prepares me. Through difficult times, I've learned that worship lets me reach out to a caring Father who hears my needs and hopes.

I feel God's presence at work, actively transforming situations and creating new opportunities. While prayer remains vital, I also understand the importance of being ready to accept and embrace God's plans as they unfold.

Fasting is more than just refraining from food; it serves as an intentional spiritual practice that opens the heart and mind to God's transformative work within me, fostering deeper growth and connection.

Throughout fasting, I've seen old habits fade, distractions diminish, and my spiritual perception sharpen. It functions like mental decluttering, allowing God's voice to be more unmistakable in my soul.

Fasting enhances my humility by reminding me of my dependence on the Lord. It also deepens my awareness of His divine power and guidance, opening my heart to His work and wisdom.

Through dedicated prayer and fasting, I found greater clarity, inner peace, and renewed strength. My journal reflects how God's guidance aligns with my preparedness, illustrating the ongoing connection between my spiritual practices and divine direction.

In unison, prayer and fasting serve as my dual engines, propelling me toward God's purpose and equipping me for future challenges and callings.

When combined:

- faith rises
- clarity comes
- breakthrough accelerates
- burdens lift

- wisdom flows
- courage strengthens
- purpose sharpens

Scripture shows that breakthroughs often come from fasting and prayer, with believers seeking God during crucial times for deliverance, guidance, or renewal.

Moses, Esther, Daniel, and Jesus all practiced fasting and prayer as spiritual disciplines before making major decisions or taking significant actions.

These examples demonstrate that fasting and sincere prayer, combined, help believers gain wisdom, strength, and breakthroughs beyond their own abilities, highlighting the importance of trusting in divine intervention for spiritual growth.

From my experience, this combination relieves burdens, brings clarity, and awakens courage, mirroring the transformative breakthroughs seen in saints throughout biblical history.

Conclusion: Fasting and Prayer are the Believer's Twin Engines

Fasting is the flame, and prayer is the oxygen that feeds it. Combined, they fuel spiritual growth, clarity, and responsiveness to God's calling.

Fasting without prayer mainly disciplines the body and doesn't benefit the spirit. While prayer can become just a routine, fasting brings greater intensity and concentration.

Fasting and prayer complement each other effectively, offering spiritual strength and clarity. They support me in making thoughtful decisions, help me stay calm and centered during stressful times, and assist in rediscovering my purpose when I feel lost or uncertain about my path.

When I fast and pray earnestly, seeking guidance, breakthroughs, or a deeper sense of God's presence, I truly feel His strength and comfort surround me, providing reassurance and spiritual renewal.

Fasting and prayer help me overcome internal barriers, strengthen my conviction, and deepen my relationship with God, making each step more deliberate and courageous.

When you unite them, you enter the realm of:
- transformation
- revelation
- breakthrough
- deliverance
- spiritual authority
- divine intimacy

This divine partnership will significantly deepen and expand your relationship with God, profoundly enriching your spiritual journey throughout your life.

Through this divine partnership, I find my relationship with God deepening and becoming more meaningful, greatly enriching my spiritual journey at every stage of my life.

Each time I combine fasting and prayer, I discover new levels of faith and a more profound sense of closeness to Him, which continually guides me toward greater purpose and fulfillment in my life.

© 2026 Dr. Thomas L. Driver, Ph.D., DMIN. All Rights Reserved.
Published by TLDM Evangelistic Media Network

Chapter 9:
What Happens to Your Body When You Fast:
Physical, Mental, and Emotional Benefits of Consecration

Fasting supports physical healing and renewal in various ways. Some notable examples include:

- **Lowered insulin levels:** During fasting, the body's insulin levels decrease, which can improve insulin sensitivity and support healthy blood sugar regulation.

- **Reduced inflammation:** Fasting helps decrease inflammation, which may lower the risk of chronic diseases and promote overall bodily healing.

- **Digestive rest and repair:** By abstaining from food for a period, the digestive system has time to rest and heal, potentially improving gut health and nutrient absorption.

- **Toxin elimination:** Fasting encourages the body to flush out toxins, helping to cleanse the system and enhance cellular function.

- **Cell regeneration:** Fasting can stimulate autophagy, a process where the body breaks down and recycles old or damaged cells, promoting renewal and preserving tissue health.

These physical benefits promote healing and rejuvenation, while also reinforcing and strengthening the vessel to facilitate and support ongoing spiritual growth and development.

This chapter explores in detail the physical, mental, and emotional benefits of fasting. While these advantages do not replace the spiritual significance of fasting, they work alongside it to enhance the overall experience and understanding of its importance.

Maintaining a healthy, alert, and energized body can help individuals engage more fully and effectively in prayer, worship, and active participation in Kingdom activities, fostering spiritual growth and community involvement.

1. Fasting Recalibrates the Body

The human body has a built-in rhythm, moving through regular cycles of rest, renewal, and cleansing to support long-term health and energy. Modern lifestyles, however, can easily disturb this natural balance.

Modern life constantly exposes us to a wide array of stimuli, such as frequent eating, consumption of processed foods, exposure to various chemicals, and relentless stress, all of which can significantly disrupt our body's natural cycles and balance. These disruptions can affect our sleep patterns, hormone production, immune function, and overall well-being, highlighting the impact of modern lifestyles on our health.

Building a fasting routine required patience and dedication. Initially, my body needed time to gradually adapt to the new eating patterns and rest schedule, as it adjusted to the changes in my daily habits.

In the beginning, it was quite challenging as I worked to manage my cravings and develop a consistent, disciplined routine. Over time, I gradually observed modest but meaningful improvements in my energy levels and overall health, which motivated me to keep going.

Over time, the numerous benefits of fasting proved priceless. My body gradually began to detoxify and regain balance, with each fasting session actively supporting the body's natural healing processes and promoting cell renewal, leading to improved overall health and vitality.

Regular fasting has improved my physical strength and overall health, while also boosting my energy and resilience. It also enables me to handle daily stress and life's challenges more effectively, promoting a more balanced and healthy lifestyle.

This discipline improved my health, providing better mental clarity, emotional balance, and peace. Though it took ongoing effort, the benefits exceeded expectations and positively affected many aspects of my life.

Physical Shifts During Fasting

- insulin levels drop
- inflammation decreases
- digestion rests and heals
- toxins flush from the system
- blood sugar stabilizes
- the immune system resets
- energy becomes steadier

Fasting puts the body in a state God designed for recovery. When you fast, your body enters a period of rest and renewal, enabling essential healing processes.

During this period, the body experiences notable health changes. Insulin levels decrease, aiding blood sugar regulation and potentially lowering the risk of metabolic disorders. Inflammation also diminishes, supporting overall health and reducing the likelihood of chronic diseases.

Your digestion gets a chance to rest and repair, improving gut function. Toxins are flushed out, providing your cells with a fresh start, while your immune system resets and becomes more effective at fighting off illnesses.

These amazing processes not only improve your physical health but also enhance mental clarity and emotional balance, making you feel more vibrant and centered.

By intentionally giving your body this time to recover, you support the natural rhythms God created, helping you feel more energized, focused, and resilient.

2. The Body Burns Stored Fat for Fuel

When you stop eating, your body transitions from relying on the immediate energy from recently consumed food to using stored fat reserves.

This natural, inherent process developed over time to enhance survival by regulating the body's functions. It helps you sustain your energy during periods of fasting or reduced food intake, ensuring your body can continue to function effectively even in times of scarcity.

It also plays a crucial role in sustaining overall health by managing energy balance, aiding metabolic functions, and supporting the proper operation of various bodily systems.

This process, known as **ketosis**, brings:
- stable energy
- mental clarity
- reduced cravings
- weight loss
- improved metabolic function

My Reflection

My 18:6 intermittent fasting lifestyle has significantly improved my health and overall well-being. By combining this fasting approach with my dedication to clean eating and syncing it with my spiritual fasting practices, I have lost over 50 pounds.

This change has significantly improved my physical health, leading to better fitness and stamina. Additionally, it has enhanced my mental clarity, increased my energy, and strengthened my overall sense of balance and well-being.

Over time, these combined practices have cultivated a sense of balance and renewed purpose in my daily routine, significantly strengthening my mental and physical well-being.

This, in turn, has greatly enhanced my overall quality of life, allowing me to approach each day with increased clarity, motivation, and resilience.

Many of my pains, persistent fatigue, and physical stress gradually eased, resulting in a lighter, more agile body and a sharper, more focused mind.

Furthermore, my spirit became more energized and aligned with my renewed health journey, fostering a comprehensive sense of balance, wellness, and vitality that permeated all aspects of my life.

© 2026 Dr. Thomas L. Driver, Ph.D., DMIN. All Rights Reserved.
Published by TLDM Evangelistic Media Network

3. Fasting Supports Heart Health and Longevity

Studies show that fasting:

- improves cholesterol
- reduces blood pressure
- lowers blood sugar levels
- supports a healthy heart rhythm
- decreases risk of chronic disease

The heart becomes more efficient, able to pump blood more effectively throughout the body. As a result, blood flow improves significantly, delivering oxygen and essential nutrients to tissues more quickly and consistently.

Fasting has historically been linked to concepts of life, vitality, and spiritual renewal. Modern scientific studies now support these traditional views, indicating that fasting can provide numerous health advantages, including improved metabolic function, cellular repair, and increased energy.

4. Fasting Reduces Inflammation and Promotes Healing

Inflammation often plays a significant role in a wide range of health issues, including chronic conditions such as arthritis and autoimmune disorders, as well as symptoms like joint pain, headaches, and fatigue. It can contribute to the severity and progression of these ailments, impacting overall well-being.

After my doctor informed me that I had elevated inflammation markers, she emphasized the importance of adjusting my diet to help address the issue. However, as I learned more about the benefits of fasting, I realized that understanding these advantages was the answer I truly needed.

Fasting naturally decreases inflammation and boosts overall health, giving me both the motivation and the practical means to take control of my health.

When your body isn't constantly digesting food, it can redirect its energy toward healing and repair. This energy shift supports your recovery, promotes optimal health, and helps you feel your best overall.

Autophagy: The Body's Clean-Up Process

Autophagy is an essential biological process in our bodies that involves the breakdown and removal of damaged cells and cellular debris.

This process typically begins after several hours of fasting, when the body's energy reserves from food are depleted, and it starts looking for alternative sources of fuel.

Most scientific studies suggest that autophagy becomes more active after 12–16 hours of fasting, though the exact timing can vary by individual metabolism and dietary habits.

This fasting window is crucial because it creates the right conditions for autophagy to happen. When the body isn't digesting food, energy shifts from digestion to repair and maintenance.

Continued fasting boosts autophagy, clearing toxins and damaged cells while aiding tissue repair. This process benefits immunity, slows aging, and promotes healing.

Allowing longer fasting intervals between meals promotes autophagy, a natural process where the body breaks down and recycles damaged cells and proteins.

This process is essential for optimizing the health benefits of fasting, including cellular renewal, improved metabolic health, and disease prevention.

This process recycles cellular components, such as proteins and organelles, and is essential for maintaining cellular health.

By cleaning up nonfunctional parts, autophagy boosts immune function, prevents harmful material accumulation, and significantly supports overall health and well-being:

- removes toxins
- eliminates damaged cells
- repairs tissues
- regenerates organs
- slows aging

During fasting, many people experience increased energy, better focus, improved mental clarity, and greater physical stamina. Autophagy is a well-organized cellular process that cleanses cells by removing damaged parts, recycling materials, and supporting cell health.

It operates continuously to identify, break down, and remove damaged or dysfunctional cellular components, thereby preserving overall cellular health and ensuring proper functioning of your body's tissues and organs.

5. Fasting Improves Mental Clarity

Many people are surprised to learn that fasting not only enhances mental clarity and concentration but also offers a range of additional cognitive benefits.

This is because it activates various physiological and neurological responses that improve overall cognitive function, including better blood flow to the brain, increased production of certain neurotransmitters, and potentially the promotion of neurogenesis and cellular repair.

- the digestive system rests
- The brain receives steady energy from fat
- inflammation decreases
- hormone balance
- distractions reduce

Fasting enhances:

- concentration

- memory
- creativity
- alertness
- emotional regulation

This is one reason why numerous spiritual leaders, both from biblical times and the present day, report enhanced discernment of divine guidance during periods of fasting, as it supports the development of heightened spiritual awareness and clarity.

My Reflection

During fasting—such as my annual Daniel fasts, Sabbath fasts, and intermittent fasting—I experienced sharper focus, clearer thinking, and greater receptivity. This clarity improved my writing, speaking, and academic work, making these tasks feel more natural and effortless.

6. Fasting Resets Emotional Patterns

The soul and body are deeply interconnected, influencing each other in many ways. A change in one often results in a response from the other.

Fasting can boost emotional well-being by balancing important hormones like cortisol, insulin, serotonin, and dopamine. This connection highlights that taking care of your body can also nourish your soul.

- serotonin
- dopamine

- cortisol
- adrenaline

These changes often lead to:

- decreased anxiety
- improved mood
- emotional stability
- reduced stress
- clearer thinking
- greater patience

Fasting often brings up old emotional patterns, revealing unresolved issues and ingrained habits. This is a key part of God's healing, as it helps pinpoint areas in our lives or within ourselves that need change and renewal.

7. Fasting Rebuilds Discipline and Self-Control

One of the most notable physical benefits of fasting is the enhancement of discipline. Every time you resist a craving, you not only strengthen your self-control but also bolster your spiritual and mental resilience, thereby establishing a more robust foundation for overcoming various challenges.

Fasting trains you to:

- say no to the flesh
- resist temptation
- break unhealthy habits

- control emotional impulses
- build mental toughness

This is why Paul said:
"I discipline my body and bring it into subjection."
— 1 Corinthians 9:27, NKJV

The verse "I discipline my body and bring it into subjection" (1 Corinthians 9:27, NKJV) wonderfully highlights the Apostle Paul's heartfelt dedication to self-control and personal discipline.

By embracing this verse as my guiding purpose, I commit to approaching my health with intentional discipline and self-mastery.

Just as Paul used physical discipline to pursue spiritual growth, I now see improving my health as a holistic journey—one that requires me to say no to unhealthy cravings and unclean foods, resist temptation, and break habits that undermine my well-being.

When you let this verse guide you, you'll begin to view your own health challenges as opportunities for spiritual and personal growth.

Every healthy decision you make—like choosing nutritious foods, staying active, or trying a fast—can reflect Paul's discipline and sense of purpose.

With this mindset, your daily choices become meaningful steps toward a healthier life, reflecting your dedication to your values and faith.

Paul stresses the need to control physical desires to support spiritual growth. He compares the Christian life to that of an athlete who trains rigorously and denies himself certain pleasures to achieve a greater goal.

Relating this to fasting, as discussed earlier, the act of disciplining the body through fasting is not just about abstaining from food; it is a spiritual practice that enhances self-control, builds resilience, and helps break unhealthy habits.

By saying "no" to cravings and resisting temptation, people learn to control their bodies and impulses, aligning their actions with their faith and values. This process is key to overcoming challenges and winning spiritual victory in everyday life.

Paul's words serve as a reminder that proper discipline involves making conscious choices to prioritize spiritual well-being over physical comfort, allowing for transformation and growth both physically and spiritually.

Fasting is spiritual training for daily victory.

8. Fasting Improves Sleep and Rest

As the body undergoes detoxification and helps restore hormonal balance, there is often a noticeable improvement in sleep quality.

- deeper sleep
- more restorative rest
- easier relaxation
- reduced nighttime hunger

Rest is a crucial component of fasting, providing the body with vital recovery time. During periods of stillness, as emphasized in spiritual teachings, God often renews and strengthens the body, recognizing the importance of a peaceful pause for overall well-being.

9. Fasting Breaks Food Addiction and Cravings

The Bible acknowledges the difficulty of physical cravings and emphasizes self-control. In Proverbs 25:16 (NKJV), it states, *"If you find honey, eat just enough—too much of it, and you will vomit."* This verse highlights the importance of moderation and warns against overindulgence.

Additionally, 1 Corinthians 6:12 (NKJV) states, *"I have the right to do anything,"* you say—but not everything is beneficial. *"I have the right to do anything,"* but I will not be mastered by anything."

This verse emphasizes that while we have the freedom to make choices, we must exercise discipline and self-control, ensuring that nothing, including food and drink, dominates or governs us.

- sugar addiction
- caffeine dependence
- emotional eating
- compulsive snacking
- overeating
- stress eating

Fasting helps reset and recalibrate the brain's dopamine pathways, which are closely linked to cravings. This process can reduce the intense desire for specific foods or addictive substances by restoring the balance of neurochemical signals involved in reward and motivation.

After several days of fasting:

- sugar cravings fade
- emotional dependence weakens
- appetite stabilizes
- portion sizes decrease
- food becomes fuel, not comfort

Fasting has changed my view on food, turning it from a source of comfort or reward into proper nourishment from God. I eat to live, not live to eat. When I feel hungry during my eating window, I decide whether to eat.

Reflecting on 1 Corinthians 6:12 (NKJV)—*"I have the right to do anything—but not everything is beneficial"*—I've learned to pause and select what truly benefits me. Fasting makes it easier to manage cravings and choose actions that support both my body and spirit.

10. Fasting Supports Spiritual Focus Through Physical Alignment

When your body is fully rested, thoroughly cleansed, and properly stabilized, your spirit naturally becomes more attentive and alert. This increased awareness helps you become more mindful of your surroundings and your inner thoughts, fostering a stronger connection with both the outside world and your inner self.

Fasting aligns your entire being:
- spirit awakened
- mind renewed
- body disciplined
- emotions steadied

This alignment enhances the depth of worship, making it more meaningful, sharpens prayer for greater clarity and focus, and brings Scripture to life with renewed vitality.

My Personal Experience: Lifestyle of Whole-Person Renewal

Throughout my fasting journey, which includes my time in military service, my academic pursuits, and my current roles in acting and pastoral leadership, I discovered that the physical changes caused by fasting significantly and positively affected every other part of my life.

These transformations not only improved my health but also strengthened my discipline, resilience, and overall outlook, creating a ripple effect that benefited my personal growth and professional responsibilities.

Fasting helped me:

- regain physical health
- break unhealthy eating habits
- think more clearly
- write more effectively
- preach with greater clarity
- navigate emotional trials
- withstand stress
- deepen spiritual intimacy
- manage responsibilities with strength

God designed fasting as a comprehensive and holistic practice aimed at transforming the entire person—mind, body, and spirit—fostering internal growth, spiritual deepening, and physical well-being.

This practice encourages individuals to actively engage with and nurture all aspects of their being, fostering personal growth and spiritual development together, rather than focusing only on the spiritual dimension.

Conclusion:
Your Body is a Partner in Your Spiritual Journey

Fasting is more than just a spiritual practice; it is a holistic and transformative process that deeply affects the body, mind, and soul.

It promotes comprehensive growth and renewal by fostering a deep and meaningful connection between physical well-being and spiritual health, ultimately supporting overall personal development.

When you fast:
- your body resets
- your mind clears
- your emotions stabilize
- your spirit awakens
- your faith strengthens

This is why fasting feels so deeply personal — because it resonates with your entire being, including your thoughts, emotions, and intentions, aligning them closely with God's presence and divine purpose, creating a profound spiritual connection.

© 2026 Dr. Thomas L. Driver, Ph.D., DMIN. All Rights Reserved.
Published by TLDM Evangelistic Media Network

This practice cultivates a deep and meaningful connection, enabling individuals to feel a profound sense of unity with the divine.

Through this immersive spiritual journey, they can gain greater clarity, insight, and understanding, enriching their personal growth and spiritual development.

When I fast, I notice that my body feels renewed and strengthened, which prepares me physically, mentally, and spiritually to take on the various spiritual assignments God places before me. This practice deepens my connection with God and boosts my resilience in the face of the challenges ahead.

My mind grows quieter and more focused, allowing me to receive revelations with greater clarity. As my soul heals, I sense a deeper capacity to reflect God's glory in my daily life, becoming an instrument through which His presence shines.

Fasting helped me align my spirit, soul, and body, encouraging a stronger sense of inner harmony. This practice showed me that my physical self is closely linked to my faith journey, deepening my spiritual experience and strengthening my commitment.

Fasting helped me feel balanced and energized, improving my health and self-awareness. As a result, I experienced a greater sense of harmony and balance across my physical, mental, and spiritual dimensions.

This comprehensive alignment contributed to a deeper sense of well-being, inner peace, and overall fulfillment in my life, helping me feel more balanced and content in both my personal and professional spheres.

© 2026 Dr. Thomas L. Driver, Ph.D., DMIN. All Rights Reserved.
Published by TLDM Evangelistic Media Network

Chapter 10: Discipline of Consistency: Making Fasting a Lifestyle, Not an Event

Many believers fast intermittently, especially during difficult times. However, there is a significant difference between fasting as a response and making it a intentional way of life.

While occasional fasting may offer benefits, regular practice can lead to deeper transformation and spiritual clarity. Consistency is key to experiencing these effects.

This chapter highlights why consistency matters, discussing ways to turn fasting into a regular spiritual habit, maintain motivation in the long run, and build a lifestyle that enhances your awareness of God's presence.

1. Fasting was Designed to be a Rhythm, not a Rare Practice

Jesus did not say, *"If you fast."* He said, *"When you fast"* (Matthew 6:16). This reveals expectation, not suggestion.

That simple shift in language is profound. Jesus is not presenting fasting as an optional spiritual exercise for a select few; instead, He expects it to be a natural part of our lives as His followers.

This suggests that fasting is a regular part of daily spiritual practice, not just something for emergencies or times of intense need.

For me, this reminder from Jesus challenges my tendency to rely on fasting only when I feel spiritually dry or when I'm seeking answers. Instead, it encourages me to make fasting a regular part of my walk with God.

Fasting with this perspective brings discipline, strength, and clarity, making me more open to God's guidance, emotionally steady, and purposeful.

Making fasting a regular practice, as Jesus recommends, helps me to experience transformation—not just during moments of need but throughout daily life.

It's a continuous alignment of my spirit, soul, and body with God's presence and purpose, deepening my faith and sustaining my motivation over time.

- Prayer is a rhythm.
- Worship is a rhythm.
- Scripture reading is a rhythm.
- Gathering with believers is a rhythm.

When fasting becomes a rhythm, the believer:
- stays spiritually alert
- remains emotionally balanced
- maintains physical health
- grows in discipline
- strengthens spiritual authority

Fasting evolves from being a series of sporadic efforts into a persistent practice rooted in deep dedication and spiritual commitment, reflecting a continuous journey of discipline and faith.

2. Consistency Builds Spiritual Maturity

One powerful truth marks every spiritually mature believer: discipline. Discipline serves as the cornerstone of spiritual growth, shaping the believer's daily habits and guiding every aspect of their spiritual journey.

It is through discipline that habits like regular scripture reading, gathering with other believers, and fasting become natural and consistent practices rather than occasional efforts.

Discipline helps believers stay spiritually alert, emotionally balanced, and physically healthy, encouraging growth in both personal character and spiritual authority.

Discipline turns short-lived spiritual experiences into lasting commitment, separating temporary breakthroughs from sustained spiritual growth.

Consistency produces:

- stability
- emotional strength
- resilience
- spiritual sensitivity
- endurance
- wisdom

Key figures in the Bible, such as Moses, Daniel, David, Elijah, and Paul, demonstrated a steadfast and unwavering commitment to their faith and spiritual calling. Their dedicated actions and firm devotion act as inspiring examples of genuine consecration, motivating believers across generations.

Consistency distinguishes individuals who make temporary progress from those who cultivate and sustain lasting spiritual strength through ongoing effort and dedication.

3. Weekly Rhythms: The Power of the One-Day Fast

A weekly one-day fast is one of the simplest yet most profoundly impactful spiritual disciplines a believer can undertake.

It serves to humble the flesh, strengthen mental clarity, and deepen one's spiritual connection and awareness, fostering greater humility, discipline, and insight.

Why Weekly Fasting Works

- It resets your spirit every 7 days
- It protects you from spiritual stagnation
- It builds your endurance
- It keeps your prayer life sharp
- It disciplines your appetite
- It trains your flesh to submit

My Reflection

My weekly Sabbath fast is a vital spiritual practice. No matter how demanding my week—pastoring, mentoring, teaching, managing business, writing, or ministry—the Sabbath fast provides an essential spiritual reset.

It provides a profound sense of rest, helps to renew my spirit, and offers essential recalibration that enables me to continue serving with renewed clarity, purpose, and dedication.

The consistent routine of fasting once a week cultivated a deep spiritual resilience, something that sporadic fasting alone could not fully build.

© 2026 Dr. Thomas L. Driver, Ph.D., DMIN. All Rights Reserved.
Published by TLDM Evangelistic Media Network

4. Monthly or Quarterly Extended Fasts

Extended fasts, such as 3, 7, or 10 days, provide an exceptional opportunity for profound spiritual cleansing and enhanced mental and spiritual clarity.

During these extended fasts, you can detach more completely from everyday distractions and intentionally pursue God's presence.

This uninterrupted period allows the Holy Spirit to expose hidden areas in your heart, help clarify tough decisions, and bolster your inner strength.

From my experience, engaging in a long fast has always been transformative. Every year, I do a 10-day Daniel-like fast, mainly eating vegetables and whole foods.

During these periods, I often notice significant changes—not just in my physical health, but also in my spiritual awareness and sense of purpose.

Insights for my writing, fresh direction for ministry, and new levels of personal growth often emerge during these fasts.

The discipline of dedicating several days to seeking God not only purifies my spirit, soul, and body but also renews my vision for the months ahead.

Extended fasts are more than just spiritual habits; they serve as vital opportunities for deep renewal, divine guidance, and personal transformation through a meaningful connection with God.

Many believers use extended fasts:
- at the beginning of the year
- during significant life transitions
- before spiritual assignments
- when seeking divine direction
- during spiritual warfare seasons

My Personal Rhythm

Each year, I complete a 10-day Daniel fast centered on vegetables and whole foods. These fasts offer valuable insights that shape my writing, ministry, and personal growth.

5. Daily Rhythms: Intermittent Fasting as Spiritual Discipline

Intermittent fasting is more than just a health practice; it also serves as a spiritual rhythm when integrated with prayer and spiritual reflection. Your 18:6 fasting lifestyle exemplifies a committed approach to daily consistency, demonstrating dedication both physically and spiritually.

Daily fasting builds:
- mental clarity

- physical discipline
- emotional balance
- spiritual openness
- long-term lifestyle change

When practiced together with prayer and meditation on Scripture, intermittent fasting transforms into a fundamental spiritual discipline. It supports believers in cultivating self-control over their desires and impulses each day, fostering a deeper connection with their faith.

6. Consistency Requires Intentionality

A. Schedule Your Fasts

Put them on your calendar:

- weekly fasting day
- monthly focus fast
- yearly extended fast
- spontaneous Spirit-led fasts

Consistently scheduling tasks or activities over an extended period enhances overall reliability and predictability. This ongoing practice helps establish a stable routine, making it easier to anticipate future needs.

As a consequence, it facilitates more effective planning and resource management by establishing a comprehensive and clear framework for organizing, coordinating, and allocating resources in an efficient manner.

This structured approach results in smoother operations and enhances the likelihood of achieving goals and objectives more successfully.

B. Prepare Ahead

Prepare your environment, meals, prayer schedule, Scriptures, and journal to support your spiritual development and foster daily discipline. These small actions can significantly impact your journey.

C. Set Reasonable Goals

Begin your fasting journey by honestly assessing your current situation, rather than concentrating on where you believe you should be. This approach allows you to set realistic goals and build a sustainable routine.

Remember that your consistency naturally improves through daily discipline and persistent effort, rather than by striving for perfection overnight. Offer yourself patience as you grow gradually and take time to celebrate the small victories that mark your progress along the way.

7. Overcoming Hindrances to Consistency

The primary obstacle to maintaining a fasting routine is not the physical sensation of hunger but the myriad distractions and temptations that divert attention and test discipline.

A. Common Hindrances

- busyness
- emotional stress
- lack of preparation
- lack of accountability
- discouragement
- spiritual warfare
- fatigue
- overcommitment

B. How to Overcome Them

- plan ahead
- simplify your calendar
- guard your mornings
- prepare spiritually
- find an accountability partner
- keep a fasting journal
- pray for God's strength

The flesh frequently resists fasting, leading to an ongoing internal struggle. Nevertheless, through consistent practice and disciplined effort, one can train the flesh to align with the spirit's guidance.

Over time, this process strengthens willpower and deepens spiritual resilience, fostering a more profound connection between body and soul.

8. The Power of Long-Term Momentum

Consistency establishes a stable foundation that fosters ongoing momentum, creating an environment conducive to meaningful, enduring transformation over time.

When fasting becomes a lifestyle:
- temptations weaken
- your spirit grows sharp
- anxiety reduces
- discipline strengthens
- revelation increases
- God's voice becomes clearer
- your emotions stabilize
- your health improves
- holiness becomes natural
- purpose becomes clearer

9. Lifestyle of Fasting Prepares You for Your Calling

Fasting builds spiritual connection and equips individuals for essential missions. When I was called to ministry in 1986, fasting helped prepare me mentally and spiritually.

During that pivotal season, fasting became a key part of my journey, shaping my character and clarifying my purpose. As I later launched my media network, fasting continued to be a source of strength and guidance.

During those times, I was shaped for leadership, equipped for discipleship, and prepared for specific ministry work. From my early ministry to launching a media network, fasting helped ready me for each new challenge.

My Reflection

Recently, my commitment to fasting and prayer has reached a new level of discipline, marking a distinct transformation in my spiritual journey. This change wasn't just about maintaining a routine; it was about embracing a lifestyle fueled by purpose and persistence.

As a result of maintaining this discipline, I have become more perceptive to guidance and direction. My daily choices are now informed by a clearer sense of purpose, which enhances my resilience and strengthens my convictions.

Fasting and prayer have become a joyful pursuit rather than an obligation. I now fast with anticipation, seeking clarity, peace, and spiritual strength.

Prayer offers me daily stability, helping me face challenges with calmness and clarity. It allows me to stay aligned with my core values even in difficult situations.

This period of personal development has significantly deepened my understanding of my identity in Christ and expanded my awareness of my purpose and self-understanding, enriching my spiritual journey.

10. Consistency Turns Fasting into Joy, Not a Burden

Initially, fasting might seem harsh. But with persistence, something remarkable occurs:

- fasting becomes joy
- worship becomes deeper
- prayer becomes natural
- the flesh submits willingly
- the mind embraces stillness
- the spirit leads with strength

Conclusion:
Consistency is the Bridge between Intention and Transformation

Anyone can undertake fasting once, demonstrating that it is accessible to all. Furthermore, individuals can practice intermittent fasting, which offers additional flexibility and can be seamlessly integrated into a variety of lifestyles.

This adaptability underscores fasting's inclusive nature, making it a viable health and wellness strategy for people from all walks of life.

© 2026 Dr. Thomas L. Driver, Ph.D., DMIN. All Rights Reserved.
Published by TLDM Evangelistic Media Network

But those who fast consistently walk in:
- sustained breakthrough
- continual clarity
- emotional strength
- spiritual maturity
- deeper intimacy with God

Consistency is the practice that turns fasting from an occasional event into a long-term lifestyle. It transforms fasting from a single act into a strong movement and from a simple act into a lasting attitude of commitment.

Chapter 11:
Emotional Journey of Fasting: Navigating Feelings, Struggles, and Spiritual Breakthrough

Fasting goes beyond being just a spiritual and physical practice; it also involves an emotional experience. During fasting, emotions you believed were hidden start to emerge.

Feelings that you tend to suppress or ignore often intensify over time. Unprocessed memories begin to surface, demanding your attention.

This isn't a sign of failure; instead, it demonstrates how God's gentle and persistent work is tending to heal and nurture the most profound and often overlooked parts of your soul, guiding you toward wholeness and renewal.

In this chapter, we explore how fasting impacts emotions, why God allows emotional struggles to surface, and how believers can navigate these moments with grace, faith, and courage.

1. Fasting Brings Hidden Emotions to the Surface

Many people enter a fast expecting only spiritual encounters, but one of the first things fasting exposes is emotion. The soul—our mind, will, and emotions—often stores unresolved:

- hurt
- disappointment
- anger
- stress
- grief
- anxiety
- insecurity
- frustration

When the physical body is deprived of comfort and nourishment, the soul begins to reveal its truths with greater honesty. Fasting, in this state, exposes what you have been silently enduring and carrying within yourself.

This is God's mercy at work.
"He restores my soul."
—Psalm 23:3, NKJV

Restoration requires exposure.

2. Fasting Reveals Emotions We Use Food to Comfort

Food is often used as:

- distraction
- comfort
- emotional coping mechanism
- reward
- escape

When fasting eliminates that emotional outlet, the numbed feelings and sensations that had been suppressed or ignored start to surface and become more apparent.

This can be uncomfortable, but it is deeply healing. Fasting confronts you with what you have avoided, such as:

- stress you ignored
- anger you swallowed
- grief you numbed
- loneliness you buried
- frustration you hid

God uses fasting as a powerful spiritual tool to bring hidden emotions into the light of awareness, allowing Him to heal and transform them.

3. Emotional Sensitivity is Normal in Fasting

During fasting, sensitivity increases. You may experience:

- irritability
- sadness
- emotional swings
- memories resurfacing
- heightened compassion
- increased empathy
- deeper gratitude

This statement is not meant to suggest emotional instability; rather, it reflects a significant phase in a broader journey of emotional awakening and self-discovery, in which individuals are exploring and understanding their inner emotional landscapes more deeply.

The soul goes through an extensive process of purification, recalibration, and restoration, representing a deep and meaningful transformation that leads to renewal and growth.

During this journey, your emotions are gradually learning to align with your spirit rather than your flesh, fostering inner harmony and spiritual growth.

© 2026 Dr. Thomas L. Driver, Ph.D., DMIN. All Rights Reserved.
Published by TLDM Evangelistic Media Network

My Reflection

During extended fasting periods, such as a 10-day vegetable fast or during phases of spiritual transition, individuals often encountered a range of emotional challenges that frequently emerged before achieving spiritual clarity.

These difficulties included feelings of discomfort, emotional instability, and mental fatigue, all of which served as part of the transformative process necessary for deeper spiritual understanding.

I recognized that acknowledging these emotions was integral to the healing process. Rather than diminishing my strength, this process facilitated internal growth and resilience.

In my personal experience, both intermittent fasting and Sabbath fasting have played crucial roles in my spiritual and emotional growth. Intermittent fasting, with its steady rhythm, helps me develop discipline and mindfulness in my daily life.

Setting aside specific times to pause from eating helps us become more mindful of our body's signals and strengthens our trust in faith. It's a gentle reminder to listen to ourselves and find comfort in spiritual reliance.

Regular, brief periods of fasting foster intentional reflection and promote the integration of spirituality into daily life. This approach nurtures gratitude and humility and helps strengthen the connection with the inner self.

Sabbath fasting holds special significance for me. I dedicate one day each week to rest and avoid certain foods to honor the biblical concept of the Sabbath, while also offering a meaningful opportunity to rejuvenate emotionally and spiritually.

Taking intentional time for Sabbath fasting helps me pause, process emotions, and feel renewed. This clarity strengthens my faith and gets me ready for the coming week.

Both intermittent and Sabbath fasting are effective practices for healing and growth. They deepen my awareness of God, support emotional processing, and foster lasting wholeness. Through these experiences, I consistently find strength and clarity by aligning with God's purpose.

4. Fasting Helps Heal Past Trauma

When unresolved trauma is suppressed, it creates spiritual blocks. Fasting often reveals these areas, prompting you to bring them to God for healing.

Typical forms of trauma that surface during fasting:
- childhood wounds
- emotional abandonment

- betrayal
- loss
- grief
- rejection
- relational pain
- ministry wounds
- life transitions

As these memories emerge into your consciousness, the Holy Spirit gently guides you through a restorative process of healing and emotional renewal, helping you to find peace and wholeness.

"He healeth the broken in heart, and bindeth up their wounds."
—Psalm 147:3, NKJV

5. Fasting Helps Break Emotional Bondages

Emotional bonds frequently contribute to the establishment of spiritual strongholds. Fasting serves as a means to dismantle such bonds.

- fear
- anxiety
- bitterness
- unforgiveness
- insecurity
- shame

- condemnation
- guilt

These emotional struggles diminish when your spirit leads. You become more mindful of God's truth and less dominated by your feelings.

6. Fasting Calms Anxiety and Mental Overload

Fasting often helps ease anxiety by giving your mind a peaceful break to rest, clear away clutter, and sort out its thoughts. When there are fewer external distractions, your mind can become more focused and calm, creating a comforting space for relaxation and clear thinking.

- calmer
- quieter
- more focused
- more peaceful

The Holy Spirit fills and changes the space that was previously filled with anxiety, introducing peace and renewal.

Scientific Support

Modern research confirms that fasting:

- lowers stress hormones
- stabilizes nervous system activity
- improves emotional regulation

- enhances mood
- increases resilience

God designed fasting to stabilize the soul.

7. Fasting Increases Emotional Strength

As you deny the flesh, your emotional resilience increases, leading to a stronger sense of inner stability and fortitude. You become:

- more patient
- more disciplined
- more self-controlled
- less reactive
- more compassionate
- better at handling stress

Fasting fosters emotional maturity. You cease reacting instantly and start responding thoughtfully. This emotional development is one of the key benefits of fasting.

8. How to Navigate Emotional Struggles During a Fast

During a fast, emotional fluctuations may occur as your body and mind respond to the changes. Here's a detailed guide on how to navigate these waves effectively and maintain your well-being throughout the process.

A. Acknowledge What You Feel

Do not suppress or deny your emotions. Instead, bring them to God honestly and openly, sharing your true feelings with Him. Express your struggles, doubts, and fears openly, trusting that He understands and cares for you.

Trust that He always understands and cares for you. During difficult times, turn to Him for guidance and comfort, knowing His support remains steady.

Remember that His love and concern are constant, and He is always there to bring peace, strength, and reassurance, regardless of the challenges you face.

B. Pray Through Each Emotion

Pray:

- "Lord, heal this broken place."
- "Lord, reveal the root of this feeling."
- "Lord, renew my mind."

Prayer transforms emotions into meaningful change by channeling inner feelings, allowing individuals to achieve deep personal and spiritual growth through reflection, intention, and consistent practice.

This meaningful act of communicating with a higher power or the divine promotes self-awareness, emotional release, and a sense of connection. As people pray regularly, they develop patience, hope, and resilience, supporting overall well-being and a deep sense of purpose.

C. Journal Your Emotions

Writing aids play a crucial role in helping individuals process information more effectively and recognize recurring patterns. This, in turn, supports the development of a deeper understanding and valuable insights.

D. Rest When Needed

Emotional release can be profoundly draining, often leaving individuals emotionally exhausted. Therefore, engaging in adequate rest is a crucial component of the healing process, allowing the mind and body to recover and regain strength.

E. Speak the Word Over Your Soul

- Psalm 42
- Psalm 34
- Philippians 4:6–7
- Isaiah 41:10

Let Scripture serve as your emotional anchor, providing steady stability and reassurance during difficult times. It offers comfort and strength, guiding you through challenges and reminding you of divine support and hope.

F. Invite the Holy Spirit into the Process

Healing is not merely self-help; it is a comprehensive process of restoration guided by Spirit, involving divine intervention, spiritual alignment, and inner growth to achieve true wholeness.

© 2026 Dr. Thomas L. Driver, Ph.D., DMIN. All Rights Reserved.
Published by TLDM Evangelistic Media Network

9. Emotional Healing Leads to Spiritual Breakthrough

When the soul is healed, spiritual clarity increases. Many believers mistake emotional healing for spiritual warfare, but often the breakthrough they seek is trapped behind unresolved pain.

Healing in the soul creates:

- clarity in prayer
- deeper worship
- stronger faith
- renewed courage
- spiritual confidence
- greater intimacy with God

When your heart is healed, your spirit soars, feeling lighter and freer than ever before. This became truly real for me when I finally faced the pain I'd been carrying for years, confronting it head-on and allowing myself to heal fully.

During my prayer, I intentionally invited God to enter my wounds rather than conceal them. Over time, this openness and faith brought a deep sense of peace, gradually transforming my inner chaos into calm and clarity.

As the hurt was gently replaced with hope and forgiveness, I noticed my prayers became clearer, my worship felt deeper, and my faith grew stronger.

Each day, I found myself gaining more courage and feeling God's presence more profoundly. Through emotional healing, I experienced a spiritual breakthrough that uplifted my spirit, as my heart slowly healed and became more receptive to divine grace.

10. Fasting Strengthens Identity and Confidence in God

As emotional clutter is gradually cleared away, you begin to view yourself more clearly and compassionately, seeing yourself the way God sees you—as a beloved, valuable, and purposeful individual.

You become:

- confident
- bold
- secure
- peaceful
- joyful
- free

As the emotional fog lifts, the actual depth of your identity in Christ becomes clear, revealing who you genuinely are through His love and grace.

My Reflection

Fasting has profoundly influenced my identity and worldview, shaping my experiences across various aspects of life including my time in the military, my involvement in church work, my decision-making in business, my health journey, and my ongoing personal growth and self-improvement.

With each fasting period, I gradually shed my fears, stress, and emotional burdens, allowing myself to grow closer to Christ and deepen my trust in Him, which in turn boosts my confidence and strengthens my faith.

Conclusion:
Fasting Heals the Heart and Strengthens the Soul

Fasting is not just a spiritual discipline.

It is emotional detox.

It is soul healing.

It is heart restoration.

Through fasting, God revealed the deep wounds in my heart caused by family loss and separation. During times of solitude and prayer, I felt the ache of missing loved ones and the emptiness that separation brings.

© 2026 Dr. Thomas L. Driver, Ph.D., DMIN. All Rights Reserved.
Published by TLDM Evangelistic Media Network

Yet, as I diligently sought God, He gently uncovered these deeply hidden hurts, allowing me the space and time to grieve, process, and bring each of these emotions humbly to Him, seeking comfort and guidance.

Through prayer, God met me in my brokenness. He comforted me when memories surfaced, reminding me of His constant presence and unconditional love.

During those moments, my heart gradually began to heal. It was not an overnight transformation, but a steady process where God's peace and assurance slowly replaced my feelings of sorrow and loneliness, bringing comfort and hope.

Fasting became my way to bring my pain before God, and in turn, He renewed hope, strengthened my spirit, and helped me move forward with renewed faith. Fasting prepares the heart to open itself and fully undergo this profound, transformative change.

Chapter 12:
Spiritual Warfare During Fasting: Understanding the Battle and Walking in Victory

Fasting is one of the most potent spiritual weapons available to believers. Whenever you fast, you enter a spiritual environment where the unseen battle becomes more active, more visible, and more intense.

This is because fasting poses a significant threat to the enemy's influence, effectively disrupting their demonic strategies, and ultimately strengthening your spiritual authority and resilience.

This chapter elaborates on the reasons for the escalation of warfare during fasting periods and details how to identify and counter the enemy's tactics. It emphasizes the importance of relying on the Holy Spirit's power to remain steadfast and achieve victory.

1. Fasting Exposes the Enemy's Resistance

When you choose to fast, you make a spiritual declaration of your deep commitment, unwavering faith, and perseverance in upholding your beliefs.

"My spirit will lead, and my flesh will submit."

Fasting is a powerful spiritual practice because it directly challenges and undermines the influence of the kingdom of darkness, fostering spiritual growth and deepening one's connection to the divine.

When a believer chooses to fast, this act signals a deep commitment to God, a willingness to submit the flesh, and a desire to grow closer to Him. This alone threatens the kingdom of darkness because it disrupts the enemy's strategies and diminishes their power over the believer's life.

Through fasting, believers become more perceptive, break free from negative spiritual patterns, and enhance their spiritual authority. Their connection with God's purpose grows stronger, making them less vulnerable to temptation and spiritual attacks.

Fasting not only brings out opposition and breaks down barriers but also serves as a powerful spiritual practice that fosters inner growth.

It helps believers develop greater strength in their faith and enhances their ability to confidently recognize and submit to God's authority in all aspects of their lives.

The enemy knows:
- A fasting believer is a dangerous believer
- fasting sharpens discernment
- fasting breaks demonic patterns
- fasting increases spiritual authority
- fasting aligns you with God's purpose

Therefore, resistance increases—not because your fast is failing, but because it is effectively doing its job and working as intended.

Spiritual Resistance Often Looks Like:
- unexpected distractions
- heightened temptation
- fatigue or restlessness
- confusion or mental fog
- emotional agitation
- sudden discouragement
- conflict or tension
- unusual spiritual heaviness

Distractions, temptation, fatigue, confusion, and other challenges during fasting aren't signs of failure. Instead, they show your spiritual efforts are making an impact and leading to change, possibly indicating a breakthrough or resistance to your progress.

2. Why the Enemy Attacks During Fasting

The enemy's primary goal is to distract, confuse, weaken, or discourage you in the period leading up to a breakthrough. Satan fears the transformation and empowerment believers experience when they commit to fasting, as it strengthens their faith and resilience.

A. Fasting Sharpens Discernment

As my inner strength and resilience have grown through fasting, I've noticed a significant increase in my discernment.

Now, I can recognize falsehoods and deception almost immediately. Situations that once confused me or misled me are much clearer, and I can quickly sense when something isn't truthful.

This heightened awareness has empowered me to make more well-informed decisions, allowing me to carefully navigate situations and avoid the unnecessary pitfalls that could potentially hinder my progress or lead to unfavorable outcomes.

B. Fasting Breaks Strongholds

Fasting and prayer are spiritual practices believed to help overcome persistent challenges like fear, anger, addiction, or depression, supporting personal growth and freedom.

Fasting and prayer are profound spiritual disciplines that not only help you eliminate distractions but also deepen your focus and connection with God, fostering spiritual growth and clarity.

By dedicating time to these practices, you create a space for His presence to work within you, enabling Him to address and heal deep-rooted issues that may be obstructing your spiritual growth and peace.

When you fast, your spiritual awareness often increases, and you regain inner strength. With this newfound clarity, you can identify and face the lies, temptations, or negative feelings that contribute to strongholds in your life.

When you keep praying, you invite divine intervention, which can lead to healing, freedom, and change. Fasting, along with prayer, helps break the grip of stubborn issues, allowing you to move past harmful behaviors and thoughts that once seemed impossible to overcome.

Fasting and prayer refocus your heart and mind on God's will, helping you gain resilience and clarity as negative influences fade.

C. Fasting Aligns You with God's Will

A devoted believer who is deeply aligned with God's will possesses an unwavering faith and a relentless dedication to fulfilling divine purpose, making their spiritual journey virtually unstoppable.

D. Fasting Increases Authority

You become more difficult to deceive and fully resistant to manipulation. As a result of these stronger defenses, the enemy strongly opposes fasting, determined to do so.

3. Patterns of Warfare During Fasting

By thoroughly analyzing and understanding the enemy's behavioral patterns, you can craft more precise strategies and secure a significant tactical advantage.

A. Mental Warfare

- intrusive thoughts
- doubt
- distraction
- discouragement
- confusion
- overthinking

Your mind transforms into a tumultuous battleground where numerous distractions continuously and relentlessly try to break your concentration and divert your focus.

These persistent interruptions make it an ongoing, often exhausting, struggle to maintain mental clarity and stay centered amidst the chaos.

B. Emotional Warfare

- irritability
- discouragement
- hopelessness
- loneliness
- feelings of inadequacy

These emotions are deliberately designed to intentionally disrupt your spiritual alignment, causing you to feel disconnected not only from your higher self but also from your true purpose and inner sense of fulfillment.

C. Physical Warfare

- unusual fatigue
- headaches
- hunger spikes
- sleep disruption
- bodily discomfort

These attacks are intentionally directed at your discipline, aiming to weaken your concentration, disrupt your mental focus, and test your overall stability.

© 2026 Dr. Thomas L. Driver, Ph.D., DMIN. All Rights Reserved.
Published by TLDM Evangelistic Media Network

D. Relational Warfare

- arguments
- misunderstandings
- unexpected conflict
- emotional tension

From what I've observed, interpersonal dynamics can sometimes block progress toward professional goals. For instance, I have seen situations where employees did not meet expectations or communicate effectively, leading to challenges that needed extra attention and management.

There have been instances where business partners pursued self-interest or violated agreements, leading to unforeseen conflicts and disrupting my focus.

Interactions with an estranged family member have caused emotional strain and misunderstandings, disrupting my focus and stability. These challenges can hinder my progress and spiritual growth.

E. Circumstantial Warfare

- unexpected setbacks
- financial stress
- sudden pressure
- time demands

These distractions are deliberately designed to interfere with your focus, disrupt your concentration, and ultimately lead to an earlier end to your fast.

By doing so, they make it significantly harder to stay disciplined and reach your fasting objectives, adding an extra layer of difficulty to your fasting regimen.

4. Example of Jesus: How to Fight During Fasting

During His 40-day fast in the wilderness, Jesus encountered various confrontations with demonic forces and spiritual opposition. Satan specifically challenged His very identity, questioned His divine authority, and aimed to undermine His divine purpose and mission.

Jesus responded with:

- Scripture
- clarity
- confidence
- authority
- steadfastness

He did not panic.
He did not negotiate.
He did not compromise.
He resisted the devil with the Word.
"It is written..."
—Matthew 4:4, 7, 10, NKJV

This comprehensive model for engaging in spiritual warfare during fasting highlights several key principles, drawing from biblical examples and teachings to provide guidance and insight.

First, it highlights the importance of maintaining clarity, confidence, authority, and steadfastness, as demonstrated by Jesus during His temptation in the wilderness, illustrating the necessity of unwavering faith and resolve in the face of spiritual trials.

He neither panicked nor negotiated with the adversary, but stood firm, relying on the Word of God as his foundation. By repeatedly declaring, *"It is written"* (Matthew 4:4, 7, 10, NKJV), Jesus set an example of using Scripture as a powerful tool in spiritual battles.

During fasting, the Word of God serves as your primary weapon, like a sword that pierces through lies, deception, confusion, temptation, and emotional instability.

Studying Scripture helps you resist spiritual challenges and remain strong. Ephesians 6 describes the armor of God, while Psalm 27 boosts confidence during tough times. The model encourages believers to stand firm, use Scripture, and trust in God's promises while fasting.

5. Word of God is Your Primary Weapon

During fasting, Scripture becomes a sword that cuts through:

- lies
- deception
- confusion
- temptation
- emotional instability

Passages to use in warfare:

- Ephesians 6—the armor of God
- Psalm 27—confidence in battle
- Psalm 91—protection
- Isaiah 54:17—no weapon formed
- James 4:7—resist the devil
- Matthew 4—how Jesus fought
- 2 Corinthians 10:3–5— strongholds broken

When I speak Scripture with faith, I gain strength and confidence, knowing that God's Word empowers me to stand firm and overcome any evil that comes against me. The enemy cannot withstand the truth I declare, and I am prepared to walk in victory.

6. Prayer is the Power that Drives Out Darkness

When I fast, I notice that my prayers become much more focused and powerful. It's as if the distractions fade away, allowing me to connect more deeply with God and see stronger results in the spiritual battles I face.

Use These Forms of Warfare Prayer:

- **Binding prayers** ("I bind every attack of the enemy in Jesus' name")
- **Losing prayers** ("I lose peace, clarity, and strength over my mind")
- **Declaration prayers** ("I am strong in the Lord and in His mighty power")
- **Authority prayers** ("Satan, you have no place in my life")
- **Intercessory prayers** (praying for others under attack)

Prayer ignites the power released through fasting.

7. Worship Breaks Warfare

- Worship confuses the enemy.
- It shifts the spiritual atmosphere.
- It brings God's presence into your environment.
- It weakens demonic influence.
- It strengthens your spirit.

- It restores your joy.

When You Feel Warfare Rising:
- lift your hands
- turn on worship music
- sing Scriptures
- speak praise out loud

Worship is not emotional—it is warfare.

8. Role of Angels During Your Fast

In Daniel 10, we see a remarkable truth:
- Fasting initiated a spiritual movement
- prayer released angelic assignment
- Warfare in the unseen realm delayed the answer
- perseverance brought a breakthrough

Daniel did not stop.
He did not quit.
He continued fasting until the answer came.

Your fast activates angelic assistance.
Your prayers strengthen the assignment.

Although a significant breakthrough may not occur instantly, the ongoing efforts are actively advancing and consistently moving forward, gradually bringing the goal closer to reality.

9. Walking in Victory During Fasting

You are not fighting *for* victory.
You are fighting *for* victory.
Christ has already overcome the enemy.
Your fast aligns you with that victory.

Victory During Fasting Includes:

- clarity returning
- mental strength increasing
- emotional calm rising
- spiritual authority growing
- temptation weakening
- purpose becoming clearer
- breakthrough forming
- the enemy backing down

Warfare doesn't necessarily mean defeat; rather, it signifies progress and ongoing effort—even when faced with legal challenges and disruptions in the business environment.

The resistance and obstacles you encounter in these areas serve as clear indicators that you are truly progressing and making meaningful advances. Despite the difficulties, it shows you are not falling behind but instead moving forward, overcoming challenges along the way.

Keep pushing through these obstacles to gain more clarity, strengthen your mindset, and achieve the breakthroughs you need for both your legal issues and your business. Every challenge you face brings you closer to victory and helps clarify your purpose in this season.

10. What to Do When the Warfare Feels Intense

If the battle heats up during fasting, take specific steps to persevere and grow through the challenge:

1. **Stay consistent—don't break the fast early.** The increased pressure may be a tactic to discourage you, but maintaining your commitment is crucial.

2. **Increase prayer.** Even dedicating just five more minutes to worship can change your perspective and shift the spiritual atmosphere.

3. **Declare Scripture out loud.** Speaking the Word of God can counter the opposition and reinforce your faith.

4. **Journal what you feel.** Use this time to reflect on and write about your experiences, as spiritual battles often reveal hidden issues or areas for growth.

5. **Ask the Holy Spirit for strength.** Rely on divine empowerment to help you remain steadfast and overcome weakness.

By taking these steps, you'll find that even difficult times can transform into moments of greater understanding, breakthroughs, and personal growth along your spiritual journey.

A. Stay consistent—Don't break the fast early

The adversary frequently attempts to escalate spiritual warfare to demoralize and divert you, particularly when you're pursuing breakthroughs through fasting and prayer.

The adversary uses pressure and chaos to distract you from your fast or weaken your focus, aiming to block your growth and progress.

B. Increase prayer

Spending just a few extra minutes in prayer or worship can significantly enhance your spiritual outlook, helping you find greater peace and clarity, easing feelings of discouragement, and fostering a deeper connection with your faith.

When you feel overwhelmed, expanding your practice can help deepen your connection with God and renew your sense of purpose.

After finishing your prayers or devotional session, spend five more minutes expressing gratitude, reflecting on your spiritual path, or sitting in quietness.

This short break can uplift your spirit, renew your outlook, and greatly enhance your spiritual experience, fostering a feeling of connection and peace.

C. Declare Scripture out loud

The phrase "The enemy responds to the spoken Word" means that when you verbally declare scriptures or biblical truths, it directly affects spiritual opposition.

In spiritual warfare, the term "enemy" refers to various hostile spiritual forces, such as demons or evil entities, that seek to undermine and distract you from your spiritual focus.

These forces often try to discourage, disorient, or block you, especially during fasting and prayer times, since these are moments when believers are more open and receptive to spiritual guidance.

Speaking God's Word aloud is considered a powerful tool because it affirms truth, strengthens faith, and can disrupt the enemy's tactics.

This method is rooted in the firm belief that God's Word holds divine authority and immense power when spoken with confidence and conviction.

By boldly declaring it, you can strengthen your faith, remain resilient in the face of spiritual challenges, and effectively overcome battles in the spiritual realm.

© 2026 Dr. Thomas L. Driver, Ph.D., DMIN. All Rights Reserved.
Published by TLDM Evangelistic Media Network

D. Journal what you feel

The phrase "Warfare reveals hidden roots" suggests that spiritual battles, such as fasting or facing adversity, often uncover underlying issues or motives that remain hidden.

Under pressure or spiritual attack, your true feelings and areas for growth emerge, allowing you to address obstacles and strengthen your faith. Spiritual challenges serve as opportunities for self-discovery and transformation.

E. Ask the Holy Spirit for strength

The phrase "He empowers your weakness" means that when you feel inadequate, tired, or unable to overcome challenges on your own, God (through the Holy Spirit) gives you the strength and ability you need.

Rather than demanding perfect consistency or unbreakable strength, God supports you during vulnerable moments. He offers endurance and chances to grow, guiding you through life's challenges. This helps you build courage and resilience, enabling you to confront hardships with faith and perseverance.

Spiritual strength depends not solely on individual effort but also significantly on divine support, which becomes especially crucial during difficult times such as fasting, prayer, and facing adversity, helping individuals overcome challenges with faith and resilience.

© 2026 Dr. Thomas L. Driver, Ph.D., DMIN. All Rights Reserved.
Published by TLDM Evangelistic Media Network

F. Remain calm

The phrase "Chaos is the enemy's tactic, not God's" suggests that confusion and disorder are tools used by hostile spiritual forces to distract, discourage, or overwhelm people, particularly when they are engaged in fasting and prayer.

Distractions and disturbances can make it hard to focus, find peace, and stay connected with God. While chaos confuses, God represents calm, order, and understanding—offering peace and support through spiritual struggles.

By recognizing that disorder does not come from God, you can stay alert and rely on spiritual practices such as prayer, reading Scripture, and seeking guidance from the Holy Spirit to stay strong and overcome challenges.

G. Praise intentionally

For me, worship brings a breakthrough during my fast because it shifts my focus from my struggles to God's presence and power.

Whenever I intentionally set aside time for praise—whether through singing, praying, or simply reflecting on God's goodness—I find that feelings of anxiety, confusion, and spiritual heaviness gradually fade, replaced by a sense of peace and reassurance.

Worship anchors my fasting journey, bringing me peace amid chaos and renewing my strength. It fosters a sense of God's presence and enables breakthroughs in my heart, mind, and spirit, even when circumstances remain unchanged.

H. Remember the finish line

When I complete a fast, I experience a deep spiritual satisfaction that feels like a reward from God—not just through external blessings, but through peace, clarity, and renewed strength in my heart.

Completing a fast after faithfully following God's guidance fills me with gratitude and quiet joy. It's as if I'm standing at a finish line, realizing that God's support carried me through every moment of struggle and temptation.

There's a feeling of breakthrough, where the challenges faced during the fast now seem purposeful, shaping me to trust God more and depend less on my own strength.

Spiritually, there's a deep awareness of God's presence and a renewed sense of closeness to Him. The distractions and chaos that tried to overwhelm me are now replaced by calm, order, and a greater understanding of His faithfulness.

My endurance came not just from discipline, but from relying on God's grace. The outcome is spiritual growth, inner transformation, and confidence that God prepares me for challenges ahead.

Completing a fast demonstrates that, even amid distractions and challenges, God's guidance leads to spiritual victory and reassurance that I am never truly alone in my journey.

My Reflection:
Fasting in Seasons of Personal Battle

Throughout various challenges in my life—ministry crises, uncertainty, loss, military leadership, business building, tight deadlines, and health pursuits—fasting has been my anchor. It provided clarity, resilience, and spiritual perspective to overcome adversity.

Fasting helped me rely on God during difficult times by redirecting my focus from personal struggles to His presence, providing renewed peace and clarity.

The discipline of fasting brought structure to chaos and helped me hear God's guidance more clearly, leading to both practical and spiritual breakthroughs.

While in the wilderness, fasting not only gave me strength and mental clarity but also deepened my reliance on God's provision. Through this experience, I came to realize that His grace is truly sufficient to sustain me in every circumstance.

Fasting does not eliminate conflict; instead, it prepares and empowers you to persist through challenges and ultimately succeed in the ongoing struggle.

© 2026 Dr. Thomas L. Driver, Ph.D., DMIN. All Rights Reserved.
Published by TLDM Evangelistic Media Network

Conclusion: Fasting Strengthens You for Battle

Spiritual warfare during fasting is not a sign of failure; it shows that spiritual breakthrough is happening. When you fast, you become more spiritually aware, and the enemy cannot ignore you. But through Scripture, prayer, worship, and the Holy Spirit's power, you are prepared to overcome every attack.

As you near success, challenges and opposition often intensify.

Stand firm.
Pray boldly.
Worship intentionally.
Fast with confidence.
Victory is already yours in Christ.

© 2026 Dr. Thomas L. Driver, Ph.D., DMIN. All Rights Reserved.
Published by TLDM Evangelistic Media Network

Chapter 13: Rewards of Fasting: What God Releases Into Your Life

Fasting is a sacrifice that naturally draws God's attention. He always notices a fast that is sincere, humble, and obedient. When a believer sacrifices personal comfort to stay committed, God rewards them in spiritual, emotional, and physical ways.

These blessings do not arise from mere transactions; instead, they flow from a loving Father who recognizes and values His children's devotion.

This chapter warmly highlights the wonderful blessings and rewards that God graciously offers when you choose to fast, emphasizing the numerous spiritual benefits, divine grace, and favor that come with such a practice.

These meaningful benefits are beautifully woven throughout Scripture and are truly experienced by believers who wholeheartedly seek God's presence. It's inspiring to see how dedication to God can bring such incredible blessings.

© 2026 Dr. Thomas L. Driver, Ph.D., DMIN. All Rights Reserved.
Published by TLDM Evangelistic Media Network

1. God Rewards Those Who Seek Him in Secret

Jesus said:
"Your Father who sees in secret will reward you openly."
—Matthew 6:18, NKJV

This is one of the most compelling and impactful promises associated with fasting, highlighting its potential to deliver substantial health benefits and positive effects on overall well-being.

- God sees your sacrifice
- God sees your struggle
- God sees your consistency
- God sees your devotion

And God **rewards** it.

Fasting can be practiced privately and quietly, but its true impact is ultimately unveiled in the way a person's character transforms over time. These changes may be evidenced through answered prayers, a heightened spiritual strength, and divine breakthroughs that manifest in various aspects of life.

2. Fasting Opens the Door to Revelation

Fasting produces clarity. Many believers testify that during a fast:

- Scripture becomes alive

- the Holy Spirit's voice becomes clearer
- decisions become easier
- direction becomes unmistakable
- confusion breaks instantly

Daniel received profound angelic visions after fasting, which bolstered his faith. Similarly, Paul found clear direction for his missionary efforts through fasting, aiding in his decision-making.

The early Church often experienced the Holy Spirit speaking directly to them during fasting, thereby strengthening their spiritual connection. Fasting truly enhances spiritual awareness, creating a warm space where divine revelations and guidance can come more naturally and deeply.

My Reflection

Many of my most powerful ministry ideas, book concepts, business strategies, academic insights, and spiritual revelations have emerged during periods of fasting.

These times of deliberate abstinence and focused effort create the necessary environment for profound inspiration and clarity to flow, often leading to transformative insights and breakthroughs.

God sharpened my thinking, guided my decisions, and revealed intricate blueprints and insights that I wouldn't have noticed otherwise.

© 2026 Dr. Thomas L. Driver, Ph.D., DMIN. All Rights Reserved.
Published by TLDM Evangelistic Media Network

Through fasting, I open my mind to divine wisdom, allowing me to gain deeper understanding, greater clarity, and a more profound connection to spiritual truths.

3. Fasting Releases Breakthrough

Fasting breaks:

- spiritual blockages
- generational cycles
- emotional strongholds
- addictive patterns
- mental confusion
- demonic interference

Many believers stay trapped in their struggles because they try to solve spiritual issues with only physical solutions. Fasting moves the conflict from the physical to the spiritual realm, where real breakthroughs and supernatural victories happen.

When you decide to fast, you open a meaningful space for God to operate in your life—vividly, swiftly, and in remarkable ways. This enables His strength and intent to manifest more fully within you, leading you on an inspiring spiritual path.

4. Fasting Brings Deliverance and Freedom

Isaiah 58:6 reveals God's heart:
"To loose the bonds of wickedness…

To undo the heavy burdens…
To let the oppressed go free…"
—Isaiah 58:6, NKJV

These statements are not merely symbolic; they represent genuine, tangible results that occur directly from fasting, demonstrating the real impact and benefits of this practice.

Fasting releases freedom into areas such as:

- unhealthy attachments
- ungodly habits
- spiritual oppression
- emotional trauma
- negative thinking
- destructive relationships
- internal battles

Deliverance stands as one of the most profound and meaningful rewards obtainable through fasting, representing a significant spiritual milestone and the culmination of disciplined devotion and sacrifice.

5. Fasting Increases Spiritual Authority

Authority is a divine gift that enables us to walk with confidence under God's strength, to stand firm against the enemy, and to confidently fulfill our calling through His guidance and power.

Just like Jesus did—who fasted and prepared Himself spiritually before starting His ministry—we can also follow His example to face and overcome our challenges. When He finished His fast, Scripture tells us that...

"Then Jesus returned in the power of the Spirit..."
—Luke 4:14, NKJV

Fasting strengthens:

- your discernment
- your wisdom
- your resistance to temptation
- your confidence in God
- your ability to speak with boldness

A believer who practices fasting often experiences a deepening of their spiritual influence. As their humility grows, their authority and spiritual presence become more profound. Moreover, God bestows grace upon those who maintain their humility and remain steadfast in their faith.

6. Fasting Deepens Intimacy with God

One of the most profound and meaningful rewards of fasting is experiencing a closer, more intimate relationship with God. When you intentionally set aside time to fast, it opens up space in your life for a deeper spiritual connection, allowing you to reflect, seek guidance, and draw nearer to His presence.

Fasting helps quiet distractions and makes you more open to God's presence. As you humble yourself and seek Him, worship becomes more heartfelt, prayer becomes more meaningful, and Scripture gains personal significance.

This heightened spiritual awareness doesn't bring God any closer physically, but it allows you to recognize and experience His nearness more deeply. Through fasting, your spirit becomes tender and your heart humbles, creating true intimacy with God—a truly priceless connection.

During fasting:
- worship becomes more sincere
- prayer becomes more meaningful
- Scripture becomes more personal
- God's presence becomes tangible
- your spirit becomes tender
- your heart becomes humble

Fasting does not physically bring you closer to God; rather, it heightens your awareness of His presence and enriches your spiritual sensitivity, allowing for a deeper understanding of your relationship with Him.

7. Fasting Strengthens Character

Fasting builds virtues that shape your identity:
- discipline
- patience

- humility
- endurance
- self-control
- emotional maturity
- intentionality
- resilience

These qualities have a profound impact on every facet of life, affecting relationships, ministry, habits, leadership, decisions, and personal development.

A believer who consistently practices fasting not only cultivates spiritual resilience but also progresses in maturity, gaining a deeper understanding and insight into their faith, which further enriches their spiritual journey.

8. Fasting Releases Divine Favor

Throughout Scripture, fasting is frequently associated with divine favor and blessing. Numerous biblical narratives describe individuals who fasted and subsequently received guidance, protection, or other forms of divine intervention.

Esther, Daniel, Nehemiah, and Jesus all practiced fasting, which helped them gain favor and support from leaders or from God. Their dedication to fasting was a powerful way to connect with others and seek guidance, showing their deep commitment and trust.

Fasting is recognized as a profound spiritual discipline that serves to prepare our hearts and minds to be receptive to God's abundant blessings, new opportunities, and meaningful connections.

It guides us to deepen our alignment with His divine will and seek His favor more intentionally, fostering a closer relationship with Him through dedicated sacrifice and reflection.

- Esther found favor and saved a nation through fasting
- Daniel found favor in Babylon through consecration
- Nehemiah gained favor with the king after fasting
- Jesus grew in favor with God and man

Fasting positions your heart to receive what God desires to give you:

- new opportunities
- open doors
- supernatural connections
- blessings you didn't ask for
- solutions you couldn't create

In my experience, genuine spiritual dedication often attracts favor. When I dedicate myself to personal acts like fasting, prayer, or seeking God intentionally, I frequently encounter unexpected blessings and new opportunities.

© 2026 Dr. Thomas L. Driver, Ph.D., DMIN. All Rights Reserved.
Published by TLDM Evangelistic Media Network

Every time I practice my faith, doors open and solutions appear that I couldn't have imagined on my own, reaffirming that devoted faith genuinely invites favor into my life.

Consecration, in this context, involves activities such as fasting, praying, or purposefully directing your attention toward God. The Bible features examples—including Esther, Daniel, Nehemiah, and Jesus—where acts of consecration are often followed by receiving favor from God or other people.

During these times, people seek guidance and align with God's will, becoming receptive to His favor. Spiritual discipline creates the environment for favor to emerge.

9. Fasting Brings Breakthrough in Prayer

Many prayers that once felt blocked or hindered become clear, powerful, and more accessible during fasting, often leading to deeper spiritual insight and connection.

This happens because fasting:
- breaks resistance
- clears spiritual fog
- increases faith
- aligns the heart with God
- silences the flesh
- strengthens focus

Let me conclude by emphasizing the significance of fasting. Doors that were previously closed open, delayed answers come, and once unclear directions become clear. Miracles that once seemed impossible suddenly happen.

10. Fasting Restores Peace, Joy, and Emotional Strength

Emotional healing is one of the most cherished benefits of fasting.

God employs fasting to eliminate:

- anxiety
- heaviness
- fear
- insecurity
- emotional turbulence

And to restore:

- peace
- joy
- confidence
- clarity
- patience

Your emotions gradually stabilize, your mind achieves a sense of calm and clarity, and your heart feels significantly lighter and more at peace.

Fasting not only helps soothe the soul but also promotes emotional harmony, allowing you to reconnect with your inner self and experience a renewed sense of balance.

11. Fasting Activates God's Protection

Fasting surrounds you with God's divine protection and guidance by creating a spiritual atmosphere that makes you more open to God's direction and safeguarding.

Fasting is a way to invite God's watchful presence into your life and seek protection and wisdom for essential choices. This act of devotion allows God to guide your path, provide clarity in difficult times, and keep you and your loved ones safe.

Fasting is seen as a spiritual practice to align oneself with God's will, strengthen one's connection to the divine, and seek guidance. It is also believed to offer protection from harmful influences under God's care.

Ezra declared:
"We fasted and entreated our God for this, and He answered our prayer."
—Ezra 8:23, NKJV

Fasting releases:

- protection from danger
- clarity in decision-making
- safety during transitions

- spiritual covering over your family
- God's supervision over your path

12. Fasting Positions You for Purpose and Assignment

Fasting has the ability to reveal an individual's true destiny. For instance, the early Church often fasted before sending out Paul and Barnabas. This tradition demonstrated that fasting is vital in clarifying divine assignments and confirming a person's calling, serving as a spiritual practice that helps believers understand God's will for their lives.

During fasting, believers often receive:
- life direction
- ministry vision
- creative ideas
- business strategies
- spiritual gifts activation
- clarity about relationships
- confirmation of God's will

When you hear that "Consecration aligns you with divine purpose," it means that taking time for spiritual practices like fasting, prayer, and devotion can really help you feel more connected to the special purpose and plans that God has for your life.

In the given context, consecration is closely associated with fasting, a spiritual discipline that not only clarifies one's purpose but also enhances spiritual gifts and affirms God's will, thereby deepening one's commitment and dedication to the divine.

By committing yourself fully to God and actively engaging in spiritual growth, you enhance your ability to understand His divine purpose for your life and to fulfill the unique plan He has designed specifically for you.

This alignment often leads to receiving advice on life decisions, visions for ministry, creative ideas, and a better understanding of meaningful relationships.

My Reflection: What Fasting has Unlocked in My Life

Fasting has been a fundamental practice in my life over the years, offering numerous opportunities and a range of benefits that include improved health, mental clarity, and increased discipline.

From my personal experience, I have observed that fasting has not only affected my spiritual journey but has also contributed to my growth in various areas—personal, professional, and health-wise.

This has become a fundamental aspect of how I approach challenges and embrace new opportunities, significantly influencing and shaping my overall mindset and strategies in very positive and impactful ways.

- spiritual strength during military service
- wisdom during doctoral studies
- revelation for my books and sermons
- clarity while launching TLDM Evangelistic Media Network
- emotional healing during my wilderness season
- strength during business pressures
- physical transformation through clean living
- peace during storms and transitions

Fasting didn't erase the struggles I faced, but it equipped me with the resilience to overcome them. While my challenges didn't simply vanish, fasting gave me the clarity and inner strength to confront and overcome each obstacle in my path.

This experience taught me valuable lessons about patience, perseverance, and self-awareness, helping me grow stronger and more determined with every step I took.

It emphasized the importance of staying calm under pressure, maintaining consistent effort in the face of challenges, and understanding my own strengths and weaknesses, all of which have significantly contributed to my personal development.

Conclusion:
The Rewards of Fasting are Life-Changing

Fasting is not a loss.
It is a gain.
It is not deprivation.
It is a transformation.

Fasting releases:

- breakthrough
- revelation
- clarity
- intimacy
- discipline
- protection
- deliverance
- healing
- purpose
- favor

Most importantly, fasting helps to deepen and strengthen a more personal and intimate bond between your heart and God's heart. This special connection fosters a sense of closeness and understanding that transcends words, making it the greatest reward you can experience.

Chapter 14
Role of the Holy Spirit in Fasting: Your Helper, Guide, and Strength

No believer can successfully fast by relying solely on their own strength. The flesh naturally resists fasting, as indulgence and physical cravings tend to dominate. The mind does not automatically yield to spiritual discipline, often prioritizing worldly concerns over spiritual growth.

Likewise, emotions rarely instinctively accept sacrifice, since they are usually attached to comfort and self-interest. Overcoming these inner struggles demands divine assistance and a disciplined will to pursue spiritual renewal through fasting.

This is why the Holy Spirit is essential in every fast. He is your Helper, your Guide, your Comforter, your Strength, and the One who empowers your spirit to rise above the limitations of your flesh.

This chapter explains in detail how the Holy Spirit actively works within you during fasting, guiding and empowering you throughout the process.

It also provides insights into how to cooperate effectively with His leadership, enabling more profound spiritual transformation, greater revelation, and powerful breakthroughs.

1. The Holy Spirit Initiates the Fast

Many fasts start because the Holy Spirit moves within the heart. You may experience a strong desire or prompt to begin fasting, along with a sense of spiritual calling and motivation.

- a pull toward consecration
- a desire for deeper prayer
- a need for clarity
- a sense of urgency
- a burden for intercession
- conviction to return to God
- a hunger for holiness

This stirring isn't just about emotion; it's a profoundly spiritual experience. The Holy Spirit prompts the fast because

He understands the divine plan and the blessings God aims to reveal in your life through this act of obedience. Your role is to choose to obey, while His role is to give the strength and empowerment needed to carry out that obedience.

2. The Holy Spirit Strengthens You During the Fast

Fasting weakens the physical body while strengthening the spirit. The Holy Spirit grants believers supernatural endurance, enabling them to remain faithful through trials and challenges. Fasting drains the body but empowers the spirit.

"But you shall receive power when the Holy Spirit has come upon you."
—Acts 1:8, NKJV

The Spirit's power manifests during fasting as:

- perseverance
- clarity
- focus
- emotional stability
- mental calm
- spiritual hunger
- resilience

You are not fasting alone; the Holy Spirit is with you throughout this spiritual discipline, providing continuous strength, unwavering support, and wise guidance at every moment of your fasting journey, helping you stay focused and resilient.

3. The Holy Spirit Deepens Your Prayer Life

When you fast, the act of praying often changes from a sense of obligation to a sincere desire, becoming a meaningful and motivating part of your spiritual practice.

This change occurs as the Holy Spirit awakens your inner self, enhancing your spiritual awareness and desire to connect with God. Fasting temporarily decreases physical cravings, which heightens spiritual hunger.

The Holy Spirit then energizes this deep longing within us, transforming prayer from a mere religious obligation into a natural, enriching, and profoundly satisfying experience that nurtures our spiritual connection and personal growth.

This transformation is a direct result of the Spirit's work within you, turning prayer into a heartfelt desire rather than just a routine task.

The Spirit Helps You Pray:

- when you feel weak
- when your mind feels foggy
- when you don't know what to say
- when your emotions are heavy
- when your heart feels overwhelmed

Paul wrote:
"The Spirit Himself makes intercession for us."
—Romans 8:26, NKJV

© 2026 Dr. Thomas L. Driver, Ph.D., DMIN. All Rights Reserved.
Published by TLDM Evangelistic Media Network

During fasting, this verse truly comes to life, as fasting enhances your spiritual awareness and reliance on God. By setting aside physical needs and distractions, you become more attuned to the Holy Spirit's presence and guidance.

Romans 8:26 describes the Spirit interceding for us in our weakness, especially when we struggle to find the right words or feel overwhelmed. During fasting, these moments of vulnerability and clarity enable you to experience the Spirit's help more deeply.

The Spirit intervenes, guiding your prayers, comforting your heart, and sharing your deepest needs with God—even when you can't put them into words. Fasting opens up space for this supernatural help, making the truth of the verse real in your everyday life.

4. The Holy Spirit Gives Revelation and Understanding

Fasting creates spiritual sensitivity. The Holy Spirit then uses that sensitivity to reveal:

- Scriptures with fresh meaning
- hidden truths
- answers to prayer
- solutions to problems
- direction for decisions
- strategies for the future
- conviction for areas of growth

The phrase "Revelation is the reward of a surrendered spirit" suggests that humbly yielding to God, such as through fasting, makes one more open to insights from the Holy Spirit.

Fasting deepens spiritual sensitivity, leading to new insights in Scripture, answers to prayer, and personal growth. Spiritual revelation comes not only from effort but also from a willingness to follow God's guidance.

My Reflection

Fasting played a significant role in shaping the direction of my ministry by deeply enhancing my spiritual sensitivity and clarity, allowing me to better discern guidance and make more inspired decisions.

During career changes in military leadership, doctoral studies, pastoral work, and building the TLDM Evangelistic Media Network, fasting provided guidance and new strategies through the Holy Spirit.

This increased awareness enhanced my ability to recognize divine guidance, leading to essential decisions and realignments aligned with core objectives.

Consequently, fasting enabled me to make better-informed decisions and handle transitions smoothly in my career path.

5. The Holy Spirit Breaks Bondage and Strongholds

This statement means that although people may attempt to overcome struggles or break free from negative patterns through their own strength or determination, true freedom and deliverance are ultimately made possible by the Holy Spirit.

It emphasizes that spiritual liberation—whether from fear, addiction, anger, or other strongholds—cannot be achieved through human effort alone.

Instead, it is God's Spirit who empowers, heals, and frees individuals, particularly during spiritual practices such as fasting, as indicated by the surrounding context.

"Where the Spirit of the Lord is, there is liberty."
—2 Corinthians 3:17, NKJV

During fasting, the Holy Spirit targets areas of bondage:

- fear
- addiction
- anger
- lust
- insecurity
- bitterness
- emotional wounds

- internal conflict

The Spirit initially breaks your chains, empowering you with strength and resolve. However, as time passes and your energy wanes, your spirit gradually loses its hold, leading to eventual surrender.

6. The Holy Spirit Aligns You with God's Will

One of the most profound blessings of fasting is the deep assurance that your life is in harmony with God's divine plan. Through fasting, the Holy Spirit nurtures and amplifies your awareness of God's perfect timing and guidance, fostering a closer, more responsive relationship with Him.

He clarifies:

- what to pursue
- what to release
- where to go
- who to connect with
- what doors to walk through
- what battles to avoid
- what assignments to focus on

7. The Holy Spirit Builds the Fruit of the Spirit in You

During periods of fasting, the feeling of physical weakness can become more apparent, which in turn helps to highlight the qualities of the Holy Spirit—such as love, joy, peace, patience, kindness, goodness, faithfulness, gentleness, and self-control—that become more visible and deliberate in our daily lives.

Fasting shifts focus away from physical needs and towards spiritual growth, allowing individuals to cultivate and strengthen their spiritual qualities. By depending on God's guidance rather than personal strength alone, these virtues become more evident to others, fostering a deeper connection with the divine and inspiring those around them.

- love
- joy
- peace
- patience
- kindness
- goodness
- faithfulness
- gentleness
- self-control

These fruits do not come from personal effort; they emerge from surrender and faith. Fasting creates the conditions for inner transformation, but it is ultimately the Holy Spirit that cultivates and produces the authentic fruit of spiritual growth within us.

8. The Holy Spirit Protects You from the Enemy's Attacks

Fasting often increases spiritual warfare, making battles more intense from all angles. While these challenges can be complex, it's important to remember that the Holy Spirit stays close as your steadfast shield, defender, and protector.

Remain alert, as the Holy Spirit keeps watch over you, ensuring your safety and leading you through these difficult periods.

He protects you through:

- discernment
- conviction
- warning
- inner peace
- spiritual guidance
- empowerment to resist temptation

The enemy may launch an attack, but he cannot overcome a believer who is wholly surrendered to the Holy Spirit, trusting in divine guidance and strength. Such a believer remains resilient and steadfast, drawing upon divine support and unwavering faith to withstand challenges and adversities.

9. The Holy Spirit Helps You Hear the Voice of God

Many believers find it difficult to hear God's voice because their lives are cluttered with distractions and noise. Fasting serves as a spiritual discipline that helps eliminate these distractions, creating a quieter environment.

As a result, the Holy Spirit becomes more effective at amplifying God's voice, making it more transparent and more noticeable for everyone genuinely seeking to find Him.

This enhanced clarity helps believers develop a deeper connection and a more profound understanding of His divine presence and teachings, thereby strengthening their faith and spiritual growth.

God's voice becomes clearer when:

- your mind is quiet
- your emotions are surrendered
- your flesh is weakened
- your spirit is alert

The Holy Spirit speaks through:

- Scripture
- impressions
- inner promptings
- peace or unrest

© 2026 Dr. Thomas L. Driver, Ph.D., DMIN. All Rights Reserved.
Published by TLDM Evangelistic Media Network

- dreams
- wisdom
- clarity
- divine appointments

10. The Holy Spirit Sustains You to Finish the Fast

Many believers find it challenging to complete a fast because they rely solely on their own willpower, instead of drawing on the guidance and strength provided by the Spirit, which can make perseverance difficult.

Although your willpower may be sufficient to initiate the fast, it is only with the guidance and strength of the Holy Spirit that you can remain steadfast, resist temptation, and successfully complete the fast.

He provides:

- strength when you feel drained
- comfort when emotions rise
- discipline when distractions come
- courage when you want to quit
- peace when warfare increases

Each completed fast highlights the Spirit's essential role in guiding, supporting, and enhancing our spiritual commitment and connection with the divine.

11. The Holy Spirit Transforms You from the Inside Out

Fasting is not merely about abstaining from specific foods or activities; it is a profound and transformative journey that deeply reflects and actively shapes your evolving sense of self, fostering growth, self-awareness, and personal development.

The Holy Spirit uses fasting to:
- renew your mind
- reshape your desires
- refine your motives
- strengthen your identity
- deepen your humility
- heighten your awareness of sin
- revive your hunger for God

This internal transformation truly reflects the significant and meaningful changes that happen as a natural part of fasting. It highlights how such a process leads to significant personal growth within.

My Reflection: My Life with the Holy Spirit through Fasting

No matter the challenge—whether making tough choices, leading others, mentoring, writing, or recovering—the Holy

Spirit has always provided me with strength. When facing family crises or feeling let down by friends, I found that fasting grounded and supported me.

Fasting provided me with a sense of calm and unexpected comfort, gradually shifting my perspective from frustration and impatience to renewed hope and clarity.

During periods of fasting, I experienced greater clarity in approaching situations with compassion and discernment rather than resentment.

These reflective moments helped me realign my intentions and cultivate humility, especially during difficult times when reconciliation appeared unlikely.

Although fasting did not eliminate challenges, it built resilience and supported ongoing progress, along with confidence that positive results would follow.

Looking back, I realize I couldn't have navigated these storms alone; it was the Holy Spirit, guiding me through fasting, who gave me the strength to heal and forgive.

Fasting sharpened my sensitivity to Him.

Consecration opened my heart to His voice.

Discipline aligned me with His power.

I strongly believe that my dedication to fasting is supported and energized by the gentle guidance and uplifting inspiration of the Holy Spirit, which helps me stay committed and motivated throughout the process.

Their ongoing influence constantly motivates me to improve my decision-making and maintain enthusiasm throughout this journey, inspiring me to grow and persevere.

Conclusion: The Holy Spirit is the Center of Every Successful Fast

"Fasting is not just about human effort; it is a Spirit-led journey," emphasizes that fasting goes beyond simple discipline, focusing on its spiritual essence and reliance on divine guidance.

It emphasizes that fasting is not merely a physical act but a deeply spiritual process that is guided and empowered by the Holy Spirit, as further elaborated in the surrounding context.

This perspective encourages believers to recognize that true fasting involves divine guidance rather than mere physical or mental exertion.

Instead of relying solely on willpower or viewing fasting as a way to show strength, the experience is directed and strengthened by the Holy Spirit, who offers guidance, power, and transformation throughout the fast.

© 2026 Dr. Thomas L. Driver, Ph.D., DMIN. All Rights Reserved.
Published by TLDM Evangelistic Media Network

This perspective highlights that true spiritual fasting goes beyond outward actions and is deeply rooted in a relationship with the Holy Spirit, who initiates, sustains, and completes the process, leading to lasting change and growth.

The Spirit's involvement ensures that fasting is not just an isolated struggle but a meaningful, supported journey toward healing, humility, and reconciliation.

The Holy Spirit:

- initiates the fast
- guides the fast
- empowers the fast
- reveals truth during the fast
- breaks the bondage through the fast
- sustains you to complete the fast
- transforms you through the fast

Remember, you're never alone in any situation—God's Spirit is always right there with you, providing comfort, guidance, and strength whenever you need it, offering reassurance and support at every step.

Fasting isn't merely about personal determination; rather, the Holy Spirit uplifts, empowers, and guides you throughout the process.

© 2026 Dr. Thomas L. Driver, Ph.D., DMIN. All Rights Reserved.
Published by TLDM Evangelistic Media Network

Open your heart completely to His presence, wholeheartedly embracing His steadfast support and divine guidance as you cultivate a closer relationship with God.

Actively deepen and strengthen your faith through dedicated prayer, heartfelt reflection, and selfless service, allowing His enduring love to illuminate and enrich every aspect of your life.

© 2026 Dr. Thomas L. Driver, Ph.D., DMIN. All Rights Reserved.
Published by TLDM Evangelistic Media Network

Chapter 15:
Drawing Closer to God Through Fasting:
Deepening Intimacy, Relationship, and Spiritual Sensitivity

Fasting is mainly about fostering a more profound connection or relationship, rather than simply concentrating on discipline, sacrifice, or personal transformation.

At its core, fasting is an intentional and disciplined commitment aimed at deepening one's relationship with God. It involves dedicating time for sincere reflection, intentionally removing daily distractions, and creating an environment that encourages spiritual discernment and growth.

One of the most beautiful parts of fasting is experiencing a deeper connection with the Father. All those incredible things—revelation, breakthrough, protection, clarity—come from nurturing that special bond you build with Him.

This chapter explores in greater depth how fasting not only strengthens your relationship with God but also fosters a deeper spiritual awareness, which can lead to profound changes in every area of your life, guiding you toward greater purpose and fulfillment.

1. Fasting Positions You to Seek God Wholeheartedly

In everyday life, it is easy for your heart to become divided:

- busyness pulls one direction
- responsibility pulls another
- stress steals focus
- emotions drain energy
- distractions compete for attention

Fasting serves to unify the various fragmented aspects of your soul, bringing them together and strengthening their connection with God.

"You will seek Me and find Me, when you search for Me with all your heart."
—Jeremiah 29:13, NKJV

Fasting enables you to pursue a deeper connection with God with your entire heart, allowing you to focus entirely on spiritual matters without the distractions and exhaustion that the demands of the day can impose.

2. Fasting Creates Space for God's Presence

God is always with us, surrounding and supporting us at every moment. His constant presence provides comfort and strength that we can depend on in all situations.

Fasting enhances our awareness of His ongoing presence, helping us deepen our relationship with Him and strengthen our faith as we become more mindful of His steadfast support.

When we quiet the desires of the flesh through fasting, our spirit begins to awaken, becoming more open and attuned. Because of this, we find ourselves sensing His presence more clearly and feeling a deeper, more personal connection with Him.

During fasting, believers often notice:

- heightened awareness of God
- deeper worship
- more meaningful prayer
- a tender spirit
- holy reverence
- greater stillness
- clearer spiritual perception

This goes beyond emotion, reflecting a deep spiritual awareness and genuine connection to the sacred. It shows an understanding that goes beyond surface feelings and demonstrates a genuine appreciation for the sacred in life.

My Reflection

Throughout my personal fasting journey, I observed a deeply meaningful pattern: the more I restrained my physical desires and refrained from indulging my flesh, the more vibrant and responsive my spiritual life became.

During annual Sabbath or extended fasts, I always found my spiritual awareness to be more heightened. Activities such as solitary reflection, prayer, Scripture study, or simply sitting quietly helped me feel a deeper connection than any other discipline.

3. Fasting Sharpens Your Ability to Hear God's Voice

God speaks, but the noise of life often drowns His voice. Fasting turns down the volume of:

- anxiety
- busyness
- emotional stress
- mental clutter
- worldly distraction

And turns up the volume of:

- Scripture
- the Holy Spirit
- wisdom
- discernment
- spiritual intuition

Believers often testify that during fasting:

- God's voice becomes clearer
- decisions become easier
- doubt becomes quieter
- conviction becomes sharper
- direction becomes unmistakable

4. Fasting Deepens Your Hunger for God

When you stop nourishing and caring for your physical body, a significant and profound transformation occurs within you. This change often leads to a heightened and more authentic desire to develop a deeper, more meaningful, and more intimate relationship with God.

As you become more aware of this spiritual shift, it signals a reorientation in your focus and priorities, emphasizing your spiritual growth and connection with the divine.

† Spiritual hunger rises.

† Prayer flows more freely.

† Worship becomes more heartfelt.

† Scripture becomes more alive.

† Your desire for holiness intensifies.

This longing for meaning and purpose shows a beautiful renewal within your soul, highlighting a richer, more vibrant inner life. As you grow more aware of your true self and your bond with the greater universe, you're embracing a deeper connection and understanding.

"Blessed are those who hunger and thirst for righteousness, for they shall be filled."
—Matthew 5:6, NKJV

Fasting is how you develop that hunger. This means that by choosing to abstain from food or other physical comforts for a period, you intentionally create space for spiritual longing to grow inside you.

By limiting physical hunger, fasting helps strengthen one's relationship with God. It heightens spiritual awareness, supports prayer and worship, and brings a sense of purpose. Thus, fasting is more than self-control; it promotes spiritual growth and fulfillment.

5. Fasting Purifies the Heart

Fasting reveals impurities so God can cleanse them. These may include:

- wrong motives

- pride
- hidden sin
- emotional attachments
- misplaced priorities
- spiritual complacency
- unhealthy desires

Purification fosters a deeper sense of intimacy and connection. When one's heart becomes truly pure, it creates an open environment that allows God's presence to be felt more vividly and clearly.

This clarity enhances His voice, making it more transparent and discernible, allowing it to be heard more easily even amidst the distractions and chaos that characterize daily life.

6. Fasting Strengthens Your Dependence on God

Fasting can serve as a reminder of our physical limits, especially as our bodies slow down and our strength diminishes over time.

During these moments of vulnerability, it is particularly meaningful to remember that God gently intervenes in our lives, offering us comfort, support, and reassurance in our times of weakness. His presence provides us with strength and hope, reminding us that we are never alone in facing our struggles.

Paul said:
"When I am weak, then I am strong."
—2 Corinthians 12:10, NKJV

Fasting teaches you to rely on:
- God's power
- God's wisdom
- God's timing
- God's strength

Dependence fosters intimacy by encouraging your heart to rely more fully on Him rather than on yourself. This reliance deepens your emotional connection and builds greater trust, as you come to see Him as your secure refuge and unwavering support in all circumstances.

7. Fasting Helps You Recognize God's Movements in Your Life

As you draw closer to God, your awareness increases. You begin to see:
- God's hand in your daily life
- divine appointments
- spiritual patterns
- open doors
- closed doors
- warnings
- peace that guides

© 2026 Dr. Thomas L. Driver, Ph.D., DMIN. All Rights Reserved.
Published by TLDM Evangelistic Media Network

- opportunities orchestrated by Him

Fasting significantly amplifies your spiritual sensitivity, allowing you to deepen your understanding of the subtle and often overlooked ways in which God is actively guiding your life.

Through this practice, you become more attuned to His presence, which allows you to gain clearer insight into the ways He provides His protection, support, and guidance across various aspects of your daily journey, helping you navigate life's challenges with greater confidence and faith.

8. Fasting Helps You Fall in Love With God Again

Many believers experience periods of dryness, routine, or spiritual numbness on their faith journey. Fasting is a powerful practice that can help break through this spiritual haze, revitalizing their connection with God and reigniting their spiritual vitality.

By engaging in fasting, believers often experience a deeper awareness of God's presence, a renewed sense of purpose, and increased spiritual sensitivity. This discipline encourages both reflection and surrender, fostering growth and renewal in their relationship with God.

It reignites:

- passion
- joy

- worship
- gratitude
- desire
- faith
- expectation
- tenderness

My Reflection

During challenging seasons in the wilderness—such as health difficulties, changes in ministry, personal crises, and emotional struggles—fasting became a deeply meaningful practice that helped me rekindle my love for God.

When everything else was stripped away, my attention was fully restored to Him, allowing my spiritual connection to grow stronger and more sincere.

This process not only renewed my faith but also significantly deepened my understanding of God's ever-present grace and His active presence in every aspect of my life, enhancing my spiritual journey.

† My heart softened.

† My worship deepened.

† My faith strengthened.

† Fasting restored my spiritual passion.

9. Fasting Builds a Friendship With God

Abraham was called "a friend of God."

Moses spoke with God "face to face."

David pursued God with deep affection.

It is in fasting that you:
- talk to God deeply
- hear Him intimately
- rest in Him fully
- walk with Him closely
- surrender to Him wholeheartedly

Fasting deepens and broadens the relationship, transforming the perception of God from merely a Savior to a genuine and intimate Friend. This meaningful shift encourages a more personal, heartfelt connection, allowing for richer and more profound spiritual intimacy.

10. Fasting Aligns Your Heart with God's Will

As you draw nearer to God, your deepest desires and aspirations gradually become more aligned with His divine will and overarching purpose. This spiritual journey fosters a profound sense of fulfillment and harmony within your life, as your inner self increasingly reflects divine direction.

This alignment promotes harmony in your life by aligning your actions and choices with His overarching spiritual plan. Embracing this divine purpose unlocks true fulfillment and enhances your understanding of your spiritual journey. It fosters inner peace, balance, and connection, guiding you towards a life enriched with divine meaning and purpose.

This process enriches your spiritual journey, filling it with a deep sense of purpose and fulfillment as your inner goals harmonize more closely with His divine plan. It guides you toward a path that feels truly meaningful and rewarding.

As your relationship with Him continues to grow and deepen over time, your understanding of His divine intentions and plans for your life becomes increasingly apparent and meaningful, giving you greater insight into His purpose for you and the path He has laid out.

As a result, your actions and choices increasingly mirror His gracious and loving plan for your life, guiding you steadily along a meaningful and purposeful path that encourages joy and fulfillment throughout your journey.

You begin to want what He wants.

You begin to love what He loves.

You begin to pursue what He assigned you to do.

You begin to move in His timing and His rhythm.

© 2026 Dr. Thomas L. Driver, Ph.D., DMIN. All Rights Reserved.
Published by TLDM Evangelistic Media Network

Intimacy produces alignment.

Alignment produces destiny.

Destiny produces fruit.

Conclusion:
Fasting Draws You Into the Heart of God

Fasting isn't just about depriving the body of food; it's a meaningful act of nourishing and fortifying the spirit. It's not only about enduring hardship; it's a conscious effort to foster intimacy and connection.

Through fasting, individuals seek to deepen their understanding of themselves, foster resilience, and forge a closer bond with the divine or their inner self. This practice can serve as a pathway to personal growth, spiritual clarity, and a greater sense of purpose.

This is not merely about demonstrating holiness through outward actions; it involves immersing oneself in a sincere, heartfelt experience of God, deepening one's relationship and understanding through genuine devotion and personal encounter.

This process encourages a deeper and more genuine spiritual connection, allowing individuals to cultivate a richer and more meaningful understanding of their faith through ongoing practice and reflection.

Through fasting, you experience:
- closeness
- clarity
- peace
- joy
- transformation
- revelation
- renewed love
- deeper trust

Fasting is a powerful spiritual practice that strengthens your relationship with God, making His presence feel more immediate and tangible.

Its main goal is to deepen and strengthen this sacred bond, which, in turn, fosters a more precise understanding, enhanced spiritual insight, and meaningful breakthroughs that naturally emerge from this more profound connection.

Life Set Apart: Embracing Fasting and Prayer as a Lifestyle of Power, Purpose, and Intimacy with God

Fasting is more than a one-time event or a religious duty. It goes beyond specific seasons or moments of crisis. Instead, fasting represents a way of life—an earnest attitude, a spiritual discipline, and a response to God's call for deeper intimacy and growth in faith.

It involves a deliberate devotion that extends beyond merely abstaining from food, encompassing a mindset of humility, reflection, and dedicated pursuit of spiritual development.

The practice encourages believers to cultivate self-control, resilience, and a closer connection to God in all aspects of their daily lives.

Throughout this book, one beautiful truth shines through: fasting is more than just a physical act—it's a heartfelt invitation from God to experience deep transformation in our spirit, mind, and life.

It is His call for believers to seek higher obedience, clearer vision, deeper surrender, and greater spiritual power. Every lesson—from preparation to spiritual warfare, from emotional healing to physical benefits—points back to one fundamental truth:

11. Fasting Is About Relationship, Not Restriction

Each chapter elaborates on this fundamental truth: fasting is not merely about relinquishing certain things; rather, it encompasses the valuable benefits and personal growth that come with it, including increased discipline, greater self-awareness, and a deeper connection to one's inner self.

Fasting:
- clears the noise
- softens the heart
- silences the flesh
- awakens the spirit
- makes space for God

Most believers live spiritually rich lives but often feel a persistent sense of unfulfillment. Fasting acts as a remedy by helping us realign our priorities. It teaches us to desire God more deeply than our comforts, like food, entertainment, or the fleeting pull of our emotions.

This is why Jesus said, *"When you fast…"*—not if, because He understood fasting as an essential expression of love and surrender. Fasting, in His view, was not merely a ritual but a meaningful act that demonstrated devotion, humility, and a deep commitment to God's will.

12. Fasting Strengthens What Matters Most

Throughout this journey, we carefully examined how fasting influences every aspect of your physical health, mental well-being, energy levels, and overall vitality.

Spiritually

You will find it easier to understand things clearly, gain precious insights, become more discerning, and feel more attuned to God's presence and guidance.

This means you can overcome obstacles, silence the negativity around you, and walk confidently in the spiritual power given to you. It helps strengthen your faith and promotes your spiritual growth.

Emotionally

You slowly and intentionally release feelings of anxiety, overwhelm, and deep-seated emotional wounds, allowing these burdens to surface gradually and be thoroughly acknowledged and processed over time.

Consequently, you attain a profound sense of inner peace, restore emotional stability, build inner resilience, and experience significant emotional and spiritual healing that can lead to overall well-being and personal growth.

Mentally

Your thoughts sharpen.
Your mind becomes disciplined.
Your spiritual focus intensifies.

Physically

Your body heals and resets.
Your energy stabilizes.
Your health improves as God designed.

Practically

You develop habits of discipline, perseverance, and consistency, which help align your life with a sense of purpose, balance, and spiritual strength. Fasting brings about comprehensive transformation, as it is fundamentally designed by God to accomplish this, fostering deep personal growth and renewal across various aspects of your life.

13. Fasting Is the Believer's Secret Place of Power

Every biblical breakthrough we examined—such as those involving Daniel, Esther, Jesus, Paul, and the early Church—was closely linked to periods of fasting, emphasizing its significance in spiritual breakthroughs.

Fasting:

- opens doors
- shifts battles
- breaks spiritual resistance
- releases angelic movement
- activates prophetic insight
- prepares the believer for assignment

You enter a realm of incredible strength that surpasses mere focus or discipline; it embodies a divine power beautifully refined through the experience of weakness.

14. Fasting Makes You Spiritually Dangerous

A believer who fasts consistently becomes:
- harder to tempt

- faster to forgive
- quicker to hear God
- slower to react emotionally
- stronger in spiritual warfare
- clearer in decision-making
- more disciplined in daily life

Fasting diminishes the body's physical cravings and limitations while enhancing the believer's spiritual aspects. This process transforms the individual into a source of clarity, courage, compassion, and conviction. The enemy fears a believer who practices fasting—because such a person gains spiritual authority and influence.

15. Fasting Leads You to Your God-Given Purpose

You cannot fully fulfill your calling if you are unable to hear the Caller's voice and receive divine guidance," highlights how crucial it is to be spiritually sensitive and connected to God to live out your purpose.

In the context of fasting, this means that fasting is not just a physical discipline but a spiritual practice that helps believers quiet their minds, reduce distractions, and become more attuned to God's direction.

Hearing God's voice and accepting His guidance helps a person clearly understand their mission, make wise choices, and walk confidently on the path ahead.

Without this divine connection, it becomes hard to truly recognize your authentic purpose in life or to make decisions that align with God's will. This disconnection can prevent you from fulfilling your unique calling and living in accordance with divine guidance.

Fasting:
- clarifies assignment
- reveals God's timing
- removes distractions
- brings direction
- opens divine opportunities
- confirms God's will
- aligns your decisions with heaven

Fasting's strength is in aligning you with God's purpose for your life. When you're genuinely connected and aligned with His will, doors and opportunities that were once closed can now open, enabling you to progress with clarity and confidence.

16. Fasting Cultivates a Life of Discipline and Holiness

Holiness is not accidental.
It is intentional.
It is practiced.
It is protected.
It is strengthened.

Fasting is one of God's tools to:

- subdue the flesh
- refine desires
- remove impurities
- renew the mind
- deepen repentance
- produce the fruit of the Spirit

A fasting lifestyle promotes holiness, emphasizing spiritual alignment over perfection. Through fasting, individuals can realign themselves with God's original plan for their lives, strengthening their relationship with the divine and fostering a profound sense of harmony with God's purpose.

17. Fasting Teaches Dependence on the Holy Spirit

If this book teaches you nothing else, let it be this undeniably clear: fasting is not something you achieve solely through sheer willpower or personal strength. It involves understanding your body and sometimes requires support, patience, and proper guidance.

Fasting is a spiritual discipline that depends entirely on the Holy Spirit, who initiates, sustains, and guides you through prayer and Scripture, gives you strength, and helps you overcome challenges. It is a process of relying more deeply on God for direction and empowerment.

You cannot fast in your own strength.

The Holy Spirit:
- initiates the fast
- sustains the fast
- guides your prayers
- strengthens your resolve
- comforts your emotions
- protects you from attack
- illuminates the Scriptures
- helps you finish well

Fasting is no longer a burden when the Spirit becomes your primary source of strength and guidance, providing the support and resilience you need to endure and find purpose in your fasting journey.

18. Fasting Is a Witness of Your Faith

The believer who fasts demonstrates:
- humility
- devotion
- obedience
- surrender
- hungering for God
- seriousness about spiritual growth

In a society obsessed with pleasure and constant distraction, fasting emerges as a bold act that confronts the urge for instant and superficial gratification.

© 2026 Dr. Thomas L. Driver, Ph.D., DMIN. All Rights Reserved.
Published by TLDM Evangelistic Media Network

It challenges society's widespread materialism and superficial pursuits by opposing the never-ending cycle of indulgence. Through disciplined abstention, fasting demonstrates a strong commitment to self-control, personal growth, and a deeper connection beyond physical pleasures.

You become a light—
a testimony—
a living example of consecration.

19. Fasting Is for Every Christian, Not Just the "Strong" Ones

You do not fast because you are strong.
You fast because you are hungry.
You fast because you want more of God.
You fast because you know a breakthrough is near.
You fast because the Spirit is calling you deeper.

Fasting is not exclusively reserved for the spiritually elite; rather, it is an opportunity available to all who are willing to embrace it as a path for spiritual growth and discipline.

Every believer can fast.
Every believer can grow.
Every believer can experience spiritual power.
Every believer can draw closer to God.

This lifestyle can be achieved through steady adherence, taking one disciplined step at a time, gradually building habits and maintaining consistency over the long term.

20. Your Next Step: Make Fasting a Lifestyle

Do not let your fasting journey conclude with the completion of this book. Instead, use this book as a solid foundation for building a sustainable lifestyle in which fasting is incorporated as a purposeful and beneficial practice.

By taking this step, you are establishing a solid foundation that will support your long-term health, promote an overall sense of well-being, and foster a deeper, more mindful understanding of your body's needs and signals.

Remember, every small effort you make plays a meaningful role in your ongoing journey toward improved health and greater self-awareness, gradually leading you to better understand and care for yourself.

Start with:

- a weekly fast
- an intermittent fasting rhythm
- a monthly focus fast
- an annual extended fast
- Spirit-led spontaneous fasts

© 2026 Dr. Thomas L. Driver, Ph.D., DMIN. All Rights Reserved.
Published by TLDM Evangelistic Media Network

- prayer during every fast
- Scripture meditation
- listening to God
- journaling breakthroughs

A Final Word From My Heart to Yours

Fasting has deeply shaped my life—spiritually, mentally, emotionally, and physically. It has strengthened me during times of war, refined my ministry, kept me grounded during crises, guided me as an author, transformed my health, and brought me closer to God than any other discipline.

I am thankful for who I am today—a pastor, teacher, author, leader, veteran, and servant of God—thanks to fasting and prayer that have helped me connect deeply with God's will and stay rooted in His presence.

My prayer for you is simple:

Could fasting act as a meaningful discipline that deepens your relationship with God, enhances your understanding of divine purpose, reinforces your spiritual authority, and invites the Holy Spirit's presence and power to fill, transform, and empower your life?

May your desire for God surpass your longing for anything this world has to offer, so that your hunger for divine presence and spiritual fulfillment exceeds all earthly pursuits.

© 2026 Dr. Thomas L. Driver, Ph.D., DMIN. All Rights Reserved.
Published by TLDM Evangelistic Media Network

May your spirit rise above your flesh.

May your life reflect the glory of the One who calls you.

And may every fast draw you closer to the heart of Christ.

God invites you to live a life set apart from worldly pursuits, surrendered to His will, empowered by the Holy Spirit, and reflecting His love, mercy, and grace.

Now walk in it.

© 2026 Dr. Thomas L. Driver, Ph.D., DMIN. All Rights Reserved.
Published by TLDM Evangelistic Media Network

Chapter 16:
Menu Guide 1
The Biblical Daniel Diet
(Daniel 1 & Daniel 10)

The Daniel fast was Daniel's way to show commitment to God by eating only vegetables, legumes, and water and avoiding rich foods, meat, wine, and sweets to maintain spiritual purity.

This act of discipline enabled Daniel to distinguish himself from Babylonian customs, demonstrating his unwavering commitment to his faith by refusing to compromise his principles and avoiding defilement through the consumption of the king's food.

Through this fast, Daniel sought to deepen his relationship with God, express his dependence on Him, and align himself with God's will. The fast also served as a means for Daniel to invite God's wisdom, favor, and presence into his life, ultimately strengthening his spiritual authority and testimony among his peers.

Biblical Foundation

- **Daniel 1:12**—*"Please test your servants for 10 days and let them give us vegetables to eat and water to drink."*
- **Daniel 10:3**—*"I ate no pleasant food, no meat or wine... nor did I anoint myself at all."*

General Principles

- **Whole foods only**
- **Plants only** (vegetables, fruits, legumes, nuts, seeds, whole grains)
- **No animal products**
- **No processed foods**
- **No sweeteners** (sugar, honey, molasses, syrups)
- **No leavened bread**
- **Only water to drink** (unsweetened herbal teas optional)
- **No oils** except minimal olive, coconut, or avocado oil

Approved Foods

Vegetables (All Forms)

Fresh, frozen, sautéed, or steamed

- Leafy greens
- Broccoli, cauliflower
- Green beans

© 2026 Dr. Thomas L. Driver, Ph.D., DMIN. All Rights Reserved.
Published by TLDM Evangelistic Media Network

- Squash, zucchini
- Carrots, celery
- Peppers
- Onions, garlic
- Sweet potatoes
- Cabbage
- Tomatoes

Legumes
- Black beans
- Lentils
- Chickpeas
- Split peas
- Pinto beans
- Kidney beans

Whole Grains (Unleavened)
- Brown rice
- Quinoa
- Millet
- Oats (plain)
- Barley

Fruits
- Apples

- Berries
- Bananas
- Grapes
- Melons
- Citrus
- Kiwi

Nuts & Seeds

(Unsalted, unroasted)
- Almonds
- Walnuts
- Pecans
- Chia seeds
- Sunflower seeds
- Pumpkin seeds

Healthy Oils (Light Use)

- Extra virgin olive oil
- Avocado oil
- Coconut oil

Beverages

- **Water only** as the primary drink
- Unsweetened herbal tea optional

© 2026 Dr. Thomas L. Driver, Ph.D., DMIN. All Rights Reserved.
Published by TLDM Evangelistic Media Network

Foods To Avoid

- All meats (beef, chicken, fish, pork)
- Dairy (milk, butter, cheese)
- Eggs
- Bread or pastries
- All sweeteners
- Caffeine (coffee, soda)
- Alcohol
- Processed foods
- Fried foods
- Artificial ingredients

Sample 10–Day Menu

Day 1

- Breakfast: Oatmeal with berries
- Lunch: Lentil soup + mixed greens
- Dinner: Stir-fried vegetables + brown rice

Day 2

- Breakfast: Fresh fruit salad
- Lunch: Black beans + quinoa + salsa
- Dinner: Steamed broccoli, carrots, and sweet potato

© 2026 Dr. Thomas L. Driver, Ph.D., DMIN. All Rights Reserved.
Published by TLDM Evangelistic Media Network

Day 3

- Breakfast: Banana + handful of nuts
- Lunch: Chickpea salad
- Dinner: Vegetables roasted in olive oil

Day 4

- Breakfast: Smoothie (spinach + banana + water)
- Lunch: Lentils + brown rice
- Dinner: Mixed veggies sautéed with olive oil

Day 5

- Breakfast: Apple + seed mix
- Lunch: Quinoa + vegetable medley
- Dinner: Bean stew

Repeat or rotate meals for days 6–10.

The Daniel diet is a flexible approach to spiritual and physical wellness that can be practiced whenever you feel led by the Spirit or as a dedicated annual tradition. Personally, I find value in both approaches.

Sometimes, I feel a strong desire for renewal or clarity in my life, which prompts me to adopt the Daniel diet spontaneously, trusting my spiritual intuition to determine the right timing for this change.

© 2026 Dr. Thomas L. Driver, Ph.D., DMIN. All Rights Reserved.
Published by TLDM Evangelistic Media Network

I participate in a yearly Daniel fast to reset my habits and deepen my spiritual connection. This practice offers flexibility, allowing me to harmonize with my personal rhythms and faith.

By doing so, the fast evolves from simply a routine into a meaningful and deliberate practice that deeply symbolizes my ongoing spiritual journey and unwavering dedication.

Chapter 17:
Healthy Bread and Water Fast

The bread-and-water fast is a modified biblical fast that emphasizes humility, simplicity, and dedication, often serving as a spiritual discipline to foster self-control and deepen one's faith.

Bread symbolizes reliance on God's continual provision, representing sustenance and trust in divine care. Water signifies cleansing, purification, and spiritual renewal, highlighting the transformative power of faith.

It supplies sufficient calories to maintain the body's essential functions while supporting a detoxification process and fostering a state of surrender and relaxation.

This fast is ideal for:
- spiritual reset
- emotional healing
- digestive rest
- mental clarity
- weight stabilization

- prayer and consecration
- short-term breakthrough

Purpose of the Bread and Water Fast

Spiritual Purposes
- Focus on Jesus—the Bread of Life (*John 6:35*)
- Reduce fleshly appetites
- Increase dependence on God
- Heighten spiritual sensing
- Deepen prayer and Scripture meditation

Physical Benefits
- Stabilizes blood sugar
- Resets hunger hormones
- Reduces inflammation
- Allows digestion to rest
- Provides steady energy
- Prevents muscle breakdown

Emotional Benefits
- Clears mental fog
- Reduces anxiety
- Helps break emotional eating
- Improves focus and grounding

Best Breads for This Fast (And Why)

Bread should be simple, whole, and minimally processed. It is advisable to avoid commercial varieties, as they often contain added sugars, preservatives, chemicals, and enriched wheat that may interfere with fasting. Therefore, during a fast, it is essential to select bread made from basic, natural ingredients.

Choose whole grains in their natural, unprocessed form, and avoid commercial breads that contain added sugars, preservatives, chemicals, or refined wheat, as these ingredients can diminish the benefits of fasting.

These ingredients may raise blood sugar, disrupt digestion, and reduce fasting effectiveness. Opting for simple, minimally processed bread can benefit your overall health and help sustain steady energy during fasting.

Recommended Breads

These options are clean, biblical, and support fasting:

A. Whole-Grain, Stone-Milled Bread (Best Overall Choice)

Why:
- No preservatives
- Higher fiber
- Slower digestion
- Sustains energy

- Nutrient-dense

Look for:
- 100% whole grain
- No added sugar
- No seed oils

Brands:
- Dave's Killer Bread (sugar-free option)
- Ezekiel Bread (sprouted grain)
- Local bakery whole-grain loaves

B. Ezekiel Sprouted Grain Bread

Based on Ezekiel 4:9 (sprouted wheat, barley, beans, lentils, millet, spelt)

Why:
- Complete protein profile
- High fiber
- Very clean ingredients
- Ideal for spiritual fasts

This is the *gold standard* for biblical fasting.

C. Homemade Unleavened Bread

Simple ingredients:
- Whole-wheat flour
- Olive oil

- Water
- Sea salt

Why:
- No leaven = humility in Scripture
- No additives
- Easy to digest

D. Homemade Sourdough (Traditional, Not Commercial)

Why:
- Natural fermentation
- Easier digestion
- High mineral availability
- No commercial yeast
- Supports gut health

Look for:
- Artisan bakery
- Ingredients: flour, water, salt only

Breads To Avoid

These disrupt the spiritual and physical benefits of the fast:
- white bread
- enriched flour
- breads with sugar

- breads with seed oils (canola, soybean, cottonseed)
- breads with preservatives
- sweet breads
- brioche
- commercial sandwich breads
- Hawaiian rolls
- biscuits

Rule: If it has more than 4–5 ingredients, do not use it.

How To Make Electrolyte Water (Safe & Fast-Friendly)

Staying hydrated is essential for good health. While bread provides sodium to help control fluids and nerve activities, it doesn't supply enough potassium and magnesium—key minerals needed for muscle performance and energy.

To prevent issues like dizziness, headaches, and fatigue, it's recommended to get these electrolytes through proper mineral intake, especially during exercise or in hot conditions.

Homemade Electrolyte Water (Spiritual Fast Version)

For 1 gallon of water:

- ⅛–¼ teaspoon Himalayan pink salt
- ½ teaspoon cream of tartar (potassium source)

- Optional: 100–200 mg magnesium glycinate or magnesium citrate
- Optional: squeeze of lemon for flavor

Shake well. Drink throughout the day.

Why These Ingredients?

- Himalayan salt: replaces sodium and trace minerals
- Cream of tartar: pure potassium source
- Magnesium: reduces headaches, muscle cramps, and fatigue
- Lemon: improves taste and supports detox

Avoid:

- Gatorade
- Powerade
- Sugary electrolyte drinks
- Sweetened sports drinks

These spike insulin and disrupt the fast.

Chapter 18: Daily Fasting Schedule (Applies to All Durations)

Morning (Water Only)

- Worship
- Scripture reading
- Prayer walk
- Electrolyte water

Midday Meal (Bread + Water)

- 1–2 slices of approved bread
- Water or electrolyte water
- Quiet prayer

Evening Meal (Bread + Water)

- 1–2 slices of approved bread
- Extended worship or journaling

Before Bed

- Scripture meditation
- Small amount of electrolyte water

This keeps calories low and focus high.

Chapter 19: Complete Fasting Protocols

Now here are the exact breakdowns for 3-day, 5-day, and 7-day cycles.

3-Day Healthy Bread & Water Fast

Perfect for beginners or a spiritual reset

Goals

- cleanse the mind
- restart discipline
- break cravings
- warm-up for longer fasts

Daily Intake

- 2–4 slices of quality bread
- Unlimited water
- Electrolytes as needed

Expected Benefits

- mental clarity
- emotional calm
- digestive rest
- spiritual sensitivity
- reduced cravings

5-Day Healthy Bread and Water Fast

Deeper reset, greater spiritual clarity

Goals

- deepen prayer
- hear God more clearly
- detox deeper
- break emotional and fleshly cycles

Daily Intake

- 2–4 slices per day
- Herbal tea optional
- Water + electrolytes
- Slow, purposeful movement (walking)

Expected Benefits

- deeper surrender
- sharper spiritual discernment

- stronger discipline
- decreased inflammation
- breakthrough moments

7-Day Healthy Bread and Water Fast

For experienced fasters, determined believers, and deep consecration

Goals

- push past the flesh
- intense spiritual clarity
- emotional healing
- direction from God
- preparation for spiritual assignments

Daily Intake

- 3–5 slices/day depending on energy
- Water + electrolytes essential
- Light stretching and walking
- Extended prayer time

Expected Benefits

- strong spiritual vision
- reduced anxiety and stress
- emotional breakthrough

© 2026 Dr. Thomas L. Driver, Ph.D., DMIN. All Rights Reserved.
Published by TLDM Evangelistic Media Network

- physical reset
- closer intimacy with God
- sharpened calling and purpose

Chapter 20: Important Safety Guidelines

Do NOT attempt this fast if you:

- are pregnant
- are breastfeeding
- have uncontrolled diabetes
- have a history of eating disorders
- have kidney disease
- are on medications requiring food

Stop the fast immediately if you experience:

- severe dizziness
- fainting
- heart palpitations
- uncontrollable vomiting
- extreme weakness

Spiritual fasting is powerful but must be approached wisely and safely.

© 2026 Dr. Thomas L. Driver, Ph.D., DMIN. All Rights Reserved.
Published by TLDM Evangelistic Media Network

How To Break The Fast Safely

Do not break the fast with heavy foods.

Day 1 of Return to Normal Eating

- fruit
- vegetables
- eggs
- light broth

Day 2 of Return to Normal Eating

- lean meats
- rice or oatmeal
- simple meals

Avoid heavy, greasy foods for at least 48 hours.

Chapter 21:
How to Break Your Fast with the Lord's Supper

Observing the Lord's Supper after fasting carries great significance, as it helps you to refocus your attention on Christ both physically and spiritually, deepening your understanding and connection with Him.

Begin with a light, nourishing meal after fasting to assist your body in gradually readjusting. Sharing Communion immediately afterward deepens your gratitude for God's boundless grace and Jesus Christ's ultimate sacrifice, allowing you to reflect more profoundly on these sacred themes.

Sharing the bread and cup marks the end of your fast with a sacred act of remembrance and gratitude. This moment strengthens the spiritual commitments made during fasting, inviting God's presence and renewing your faith as you transition back to daily life.

Step-By-Step Process

1. Prepare Quietly and Prayerfully

Find a private place (or do this with family).

2. Read a Scripture

Suggested passages:
- Luke 22:14–20
- 1 Corinthians 11:23–26
- Isaiah 53
- John 6

3. Pray a Prayer of Thanksgiving

Thank God for:
- strength to complete the fast
- the breakthroughs
- cleansing
- revelation
- protection
- discipline

4. Examine Your Heart (1 Cor. 11:28)

Ask:
"Lord, is there anything in me that needs cleansing?"

© 2026 Dr. Thomas L. Driver, Ph.D., DMIN. All Rights Reserved.
Published by TLDM Evangelistic Media Network

5. Take the Bread

Say:

"This represents Your body broken for me. I take it with gratitude."

Eat the bread slowly.

Let it be your first physical meal.

6. Take the Cup

Say:

"This represents your bloodshed for me. I receive Your cleansing, healing, and new covenant."

Drink with reverence.

7. Pray a Prayer of Rededication

Seal your fast by declaring:
- I recommit my life
- I recommit my purpose
- I recommit my body
- I recommit my calling
- I recommit my walk with Christ

© 2026 Dr. Thomas L. Driver, Ph.D., DMIN. All Rights Reserved.
Published by TLDM Evangelistic Media Network

What Happens in the Spirit When You Break Your Fast this Way

Believers who break a fast with Communion often experience:

- waves of peace
- emotional release
- tears of joy
- deep clarity
- spiritual sensitivity
- healing
- prophetic impressions
- renewed identity
- cleansing
- restored strength

This is because the heart is wide open to God.

Why Every Christian Should Do This

Breaking a fast with the Lord's Supper:

- honors God
- stabilizes the body
- centers the mind
- resets the emotions
- awakens gratitude

- affirms identity
- strengthens the spirit
- seals the fast
- prepares you for the next assignment

It's a spiritual discipline with physical wisdom and emotional healing.

Chapter 22:
My Testimony:
How Fasting, Prayer, and Communion Transformed My Life

I started fasting and praying before I truly understood their significance. My experiences in the military, ministry, academia, family challenges, health problems, and adversity have given me a valuable perspective.

God repeatedly guided me into the discipline of *consecration*. I did not choose this path to appear religious or impressive. I decided it because my life depended on hearing God clearly, trusting in His strength, and staying rooted in His presence.

I realized early on that fasting isn't merely about skipping meals; it's a deeply heartfelt practice that allows me to cleanse my mind and spirit. Each fast creates space for God's presence by helping me release distractions and focus more fully on my faith and connection with Him.

Every fasting/prayer episode sharpened my focus. Every time I read Scripture, it renewed my perspective. Also, each time I completed a fast with the Lord's Supper (Communion), it confirmed the work that God had done in my spirit.

Over the years, fasting has supported me through some of life's toughest moments. During my twenty-seven years in the military, particularly in remote and deployed assignments, fasting helped maintain my spirit when I faced demands for strength I didn't always possess.

In challenging periods like family separation, legal troubles, financial difficulties, betrayal, spiritual struggles, and loneliness, fasting and prayer kept me centered and strong. When faith was all I had, fasting gave me both resilience and renewal.

While I was on my wilderness journey and my life was unsettled, fasting was my way to quiet my soul and hear God. Sometimes, my fasting came from sheer desperation.

Various fasting practices—such as Daniel, bread-and-water, egg, Sabbath, and intermittent fasting—have brought me spiritual healing. Each fast has taught me valuable lessons in obedience, discipline, and surrender.

During these periods of fasting, God not only healed my emotional wounds but also renewed my strength and restored my clarity of vision, allowing me to see my life's path with renewed hope and purpose.

It was also through fasting that I overcame fear, anxiety, and insecurities that had silently burdened me for years. Furthermore, fasting reshaped my calling, refined my character, and reaffirmed my identity as a servant of God.

© 2026 Dr. Thomas L. Driver, Ph.D., DMIN. All Rights Reserved.
Published by TLDM Evangelistic Media Network

Fasting also transformed my physical health.

I lost more than 60 pounds by following a disciplined approach that included fasting and healthy eating, steering clear of fad diets or shortcuts. This journey demanded dedication and a commitment to properly nourishing my body.

My energy levels significantly improved, allowing me to feel more vibrant and active throughout the day. My thinking became more precise and more focused, enabling better decision-making and creativity.

My sleep became more restful, and the practice of regular fasting fostered a sense of balance and overall well-being that persisted over time.

The most powerful change happened when I started breaking my fasts by sharing in Communion. Ending a fast with the Lord's Supper deeply enriched my experience and understanding.

It was a truly special moment—a heartfelt gathering where fasting brought us closer to the covenant, sacrifice mingled with grace, and human hunger was lovingly satisfied on a spiritual level.

After hours or even days of denying my flesh and disregarding my worldly desires, Communion gently reminded me that my true and proper nourishment is found in Christ Himself, who sustains and fulfills me.

© 2026 Dr. Thomas L. Driver, Ph.D., DMIN. All Rights Reserved.
Published by TLDM Evangelistic Media Network

When I broke my fast with Communion:
- my heart became tender before God
- my mind settled into peace
- my spirit opened to revelation
- my soul remembered its covenant
- my faith became unshakeable

Communion sealed the fast like a spiritual signature, reminding me that the work within me was Spirit-led, not self-driven. It wasn't about weight loss, discipline, or mental strength, but about Jesus—His body broken for me, His blood shed for me, and His life alive in me.

As I deepened my commitment to fasting and prayer, God entrusted me with greater responsibilities in my ministry, expanded my influence to reach more people, and ignited a renewed passion and fire within me that continues to grow.

My devotional writing deepened, my preaching sharpened, and my academic, pastoral, and leadership skills grew. My roles as author, professor, pastor, and founder of TLDM Evangelistic Media Network became more defined.

Fasting and Communion have imparted lessons that go beyond mere spiritual practice, fostering a profound understanding of integrity, discipline, and unwavering faith.

These experiences have shaped my character, reinforcing my commitment to living authentically and maintaining steadfast trust in my beliefs.

These experiences have significantly shaped my character and serve as guiding principles that influence my actions and decisions across all areas of life. They foster personal growth, resilience, and a continual pursuit of self-improvement.

They helped me defeat the desires of the flesh.
They taught me spiritual authority.
They trained my mind for battle.
They aligned my life with heaven.
They kept me humble, teachable, and dependent on God.

For me, fasting has evolved into a comprehensive way of life—it's no longer merely a spiritual obligation but a daily reflection of my unwavering devotion, discipline, and commitment to my beliefs.

Prayer sustains me and is as vital as the air I breathe, nourishing my soul and guiding my every step. Communion has evolved from a simple tradition into a powerful reminder of my intimate, covenant relationship with Christ, anchoring my faith and renewing my spirit each time I partake.

These disciplines molded me into the man I am today:
a pastor with conviction,
a teacher with clarity,
a servant with compassion,

an author with purpose,
and a believer eagerly awaiting Christ's return.

If God can transform my life through fasting, prayer, and Communion, then He can certainly bring positive change to anyone who seeks Him sincerely and with genuine faith. His power and grace are available to all who approach Him honestly and humbly.

This is my testimony.
This is my journey.
This is my covenant walk.
And to God be all the glory.

References

Chapter 1

- Psalm 35:13 (NKJV)
- Matthew 4:4 (NKJV)
- Joel 1:14 (NKJV)
- Matthew 6:16 (NKJV)
- Matthew 4:2 (NKJV)
- Daniel 1:8 (NKJV)
- Acts 13:2 (NKJV)
- Matthew 6:16–18 (NKJV)
- Matthew 5:6 (NKJV)
- Matthew 6:5–6 (NKJV)
- James 4:10 (NKJV)
- Matthew 6:16–18 (NKJV)
- Matthew 6:16–18 (NKJV)
- Joel 2:12–14 (NKJV)
- Acts 13:2–3 (NKJV)
- Matthew 4:1–2 (NKJV)

Chapter 2

- Joel 2:12 (NKJV)
- Matthew 6:18 (NKJV)
- Psalm 42:2 (NKJV)
- 2 Corinthians 13:5 (NKJV)
- Romans 12:1 (NKJV)
- Psalm 63:8 (NKJV)

Chapter 3

- Joel 2:12–13 (NKJV)
- Ezra 8:21–23 (NKJV)
- Exodus 34:28 (NKJV)
- 1 Kings 19:4 (NKJV)
- 1 Kings 19:7 (NKJV)
- 1 Kings 19:12 (NKJV)
- Esther 4:16 (NKJV)
- Psalm 35:13 (NKJV)
- Jeremiah 29:13 (NKJV)
- 1 Corinthians 10:31 (NKJV)
- Daniel 1:15 (NKJV)
- Daniel 10:2–3 (NKJV)
- Isaiah 58:6 (NKJV)

Chapter 4

- Matthew 4:1–2 (NKJV)
- Luke 4:14 (NKJV)
- Matthew 6:16–18 (NKJV)
- Matthew 9:15 (NKJV)
- Acts 13:2 (NKJV)
- Acts 14:23 (NKJV)
- 2 Corinthians 6:4–5 (NKJV)

Chapter 5

- Daniel 1:8 (NKJV)
- Esther 4:16 (NKJV)
- Matthew 6:16–18 (NKJV)

Chapter 6

- Matthew 6:16–18 (NKJV)
- Joel 2:12 (NKJV)
- Psalm 51:17 (NKJV)
- Proverbs 16:3 (NKJV)
- Romans 12:1–2 (NKJV)
- Isaiah 58:6 (NKJV)

Chapter 7

- Galatians 5:16–17 (NKJV)
- Matthew 17:21 (NKJV)
- Ephesians 6:12 (NKJV)
- Isaiah 58:6 (NKJV)
- Daniel 10:12–13 (NKJV)
- 2 Corinthians 10:3–5 (NKJV)

Chapter 8

- Matthew 6:16–18 (NKJV)
- Acts 13:2 (NKJV)
- Jeremiah 33:3 (NKJV)
- Isaiah 58:6 (NKJV)
- Psalm 63:1 (NKJV)
- John 4:23–24 (NKJV)
- Hebrews 4:12 (NKJV)

Chapter 9

- 1 Corinthians 9:27 (NKJV)

Chapter 10

- Matthew 6:16–18 (NKJV)

Chapter 11

- Psalm 42:3 (NKJV)
- Isaiah 26:3 (NKJV)
- Philippians 4:6–7 (NKJV)

Chapter 12

- Ephesians 6:12 (NKJV)
- Matthew 4:1–11 (NKJV)
- Hebrews 4:12 (NKJV)
- James 4:7 (NKJV)
- Daniel 10:12–13 (NKJV)
- Psalm 91:11 (NKJV)
- 1 Peter 5:8–9 (NKJV)

Chapter 13

- Matthew 6:18 (NKJV)
- Jeremiah 29:13 (NKJV)
- Psalm 34:10 (NKJV)
- Isaiah 58:11 (NKJV)
- Psalm 84:11 (NKJV)
- Psalm 16:11 (NKJV)
- Proverbs 3:5–6 (NKJV)

Chapter 14

- Romans 8:14 (NKJV)
- Zechariah 4:6 (NKJV)
- John 14:26 (NKJV)
- John 16:13 (NKJV)
- Galatians 5:22–23 (NKJV)
- 2 Timothy 1:7 (NKJV)
- John 10:27 (NKJV)
- Matthew 6:16–18 (NKJV)
- Matthew 5:6 (NKJV)
- Acts 13:2 (NKJV)
- Romans 12:1 (NKJV)
- Galatians 5:16 (NKJV)
- Hebrews 12:11 (NKJV)

Chapter 16

- Daniel 1:12 (NKJV)
- Daniel 10:3 (NKJV)

Chapter 17

- Daniel 1:12 (NKJV)
- Daniel 10:3 (NKJV)

Chapter 18

- Matthew 4:2 (NKJV)
- Daniel 1:8 (NKJV)
- Acts 13:2 (NKJV)
- Matthew 6:16–18 (NKJV)

Chapter 21

- Luke 22:14–20
- 1 Corinthians 11:23–26
- Isaiah 53
- John 6
- 1 Corinthians 11:28

Chapter 22

- Matthew 6:16–18 (NKJV)
- Psalm 35:13 (NKJV)
- Isaiah 58:6 (NKJV)
- Joel 2:12 (NKJV)
- Matthew 4:4 (NKJV)
- Acts 13:2–3 (NKJV)

© 2026 Dr. Thomas L. Driver, Ph.D., DMIN. All Rights Reserved.
Published by TLDM Evangelistic Media Network

About the Book

*Fasting and Prayer: **A Lifestyle of Consecration*** is a transformative guide created to help believers embrace ancient biblical practices that bring clarity, breakthroughs, healing, and spiritual empowerment.

In a world full of distractions, stress, emotional exhaustion, and spiritual battles, this book invites Christians back to the simplicity and strength of a surrendered life before God.

Drawing from Scripture, pastoral wisdom, and decades of personal experience, Dr. Thomas L. Driver provides a comprehensive and practical roadmap for fasting and prayer—designed for both new believers and experienced disciples.

This book examines the spiritual, emotional, and physical benefits of consecration. It demonstrates how fasting helps control the flesh, sharpen the spirit, and prepare the believer for greater assignments in the Kingdom of God.

Readers will learn how to fast safely and effectively through multiple methods, including the Daniel fast, intermittent fasting, bread-and-water fasting, spiritual hybrid fasting, Sabbath fasting, and extended consecrations.

© 2026 Dr. Thomas L. Driver, Ph.D., DMIN. All Rights Reserved.
Published by TLDM Evangelistic Media Network

The book also includes practical strategies for meal planning, hydration, spiritual discipline, emotional regulation, and breaking the fast with Communion. This sacred moment seals the spiritual work God has done.

This is more than a guide on fasting—it's an account of transformation. Dr. Driver shares personal stories to show how fasting restores vision, strengthens character, and renews purpose.

What sets this book apart is its holistic approach. It addresses the **whole person**—spirit, soul, and body—showing readers how a lifestyle of consecration leads to:

- deeper intimacy with God
- stronger spiritual sensitivity
- emotional freedom and peace
- increased mental clarity
- improved physical health
- disciplined living
- renewed purpose and identity
- consistent breakthrough

Whether you are seeking direction, deliverance, healing, discipline, or deeper communion with God, this book will empower you with biblical understanding, practical application, and spiritual insight to pursue a consecrated life. It is designed to be read devotionally, studied intensely, and lived out daily.

© 2026 Dr. Thomas L. Driver, Ph.D., DMIN. All Rights Reserved.
Published by TLDM Evangelistic Media Network

This book is a call to return to the ancient paths—the practices Jesus taught, the apostles lived, and generations of believers embraced. It is an invitation to rise higher, walk closer, and live fully surrendered to the will of God.

Fasting and prayer have profoundly transformed countless lives throughout history, inspiring spiritual growth, personal resilience, and meaningful change.

Through these pages, they may very well transform yours.

About the Author

Dr. Thomas L. Driver, Ph.D., DMIN., is a retired U.S. Navy veteran, pastor, educator, and founder of **TLDM Evangelistic Media Network**, a global Christian organization dedicated to teaching and advancing the gospel through books, devotionals, sermons, and media.

Throughout his life, Dr. Driver faced seasons of intense testing—military pressure, personal challenges, wilderness experiences, health struggles, and spiritual warfare. It was fasting and prayer that transformed him, restoring his strength, renewing his mind, and deepening his intimacy with God.

Through Daniel's fasts, hybrid models, bread-and-water fasts, Sabbath fasts, and extended consecrations, he achieved impressive spiritual and physical breakthroughs, including notable weight loss, emotional healing, and renewed clarity of purpose.

Dr. Driver shares his testimony and biblical insight to encourage believers toward disciplined, Spirit-led lives. Through his writing and teaching, he promotes holiness, spiritual growth, and readiness for Christ's return, while continuing to serve, mentor, and produce ministry content.

© 2026 Dr. Thomas L. Driver, Ph.D., DMIN. All Rights Reserved.
Published by TLDM Evangelistic Media Network

More Books on Prayer by Dr. Thomas L. Driver, PhD, DMIN

The Prayers of the Prophets

The Prayers of the Prophets explores how God reveals His power, mercy, and purpose through the prayers of His people.

Rooted in Scripture and guided by faith, this book combines two profound expressions of divine communication: the model prayer given by Jesus Christ and the heartfelt petitions of the prophets who spoke on behalf of nations.

© 2026 Dr. Thomas L. Driver, Ph.D., DMIN. All Rights Reserved.
Published by TLDM Evangelistic Media Network

Teach Me to Pray
Lessons from Scripture

Teach Me to Pray: Lessons from Scripture examines the biblical foundation, spiritual depth, and practical discipline of prayer as revealed through God's Word.

Drawing from both Old and New Testament examples, the book demonstrates how faithful men and women—such as Moses, Hannah, David, Daniel, and Jesus—approached God with humility, persistence, and faith.

Each chapter explores a different principle of prayer, illustrating how Scripture guides believers to pray with sincerity, authority, and in accordance with God's will.

The book highlights prayer as both communion and warfare—an intimate conversation with the Father and a divine partnership in carrying out His purposes on earth.

Discover these and other inspiring works by Dr. Driver at:

- **Ministry Official Bookstore:** https://tldmevangelisticmedianetwork.com/tldm-bookstore/
- **Amazon Author Page:** https://www.amazon.com/author/drtldriver22
- **Barnes & Noble:** https://www.barnesandnoble.com/s/Dr.%20Thomas%20L.%20Driver%20PhD%20DMIN

© 2026 Dr. Thomas L. Driver, Ph.D., DMIN. All Rights Reserved.
Published by TLDM Evangelistic Media Network

www.ingramcontent.com/pod-product-compliance
Lightning Source LLC
Chambersburg PA
CBHW070614160426
43194CB00009B/1267